Dedication

Moaz Safi Yousef al-Kasasbeh
May 29, 1988–January 3, 2015

Also by Yatir Nitzany

Conversational Portuguese Quick and Easy

Conversational Spanish Quick and Easy

Conversational Italian Quick and Easy

Conversational French Quick and Easy

Conversational German Quick and Easy

Conversational Russian Quick and Easy

Conversational Polish Quick and Easy

Conversational Hebrew Quick and Easy

Conversational Yiddish Quick and Easy

Conversational Arabic Quick and Easy
Classical Arabic

Conversational Arabic Quick and Easy
Palestinian Dialect

Conversational Arabic Quick and Easy
Egyptian Dialect

Conversational Arabic Quick and Easy
Jordanian Dialect

Conversational Arabic Quick and Easy
Emirati Dialect

Conversational Arabic Quick and Easy
Syrian Dialect

Conversational
Arabic
Quick and Easy

GULF DIALECTS

YATIR NITZANY

Copyright © 2019
Yatir Nitzany
All rights reserved.
ISBN-13: 978-1951244439

Printed in the United States of America

Foreword

About Myself

For many years I struggled to learn Spanish, and I still knew no more than about twenty words. Consequently, I was extremely frustrated. One day I stumbled upon this method as I was playing around with word combinations. Suddenly, I came to the realization that every language has a certain core group of words that are most commonly used and, simply by learning them, one could gain the ability to engage in quick and easy conversational Spanish.

I discovered which words those were, and I narrowed them down to three hundred and fifty that, once memorized, one could connect and create one's own sentences. The variations were and are infinite! By using this incredibly simple technique, I could converse at a proficient level and speak Spanish. Within a week, I astonished my Spanish-speaking friends with my newfound ability. The next semester I registered at my university for a Spanish language course, and I applied the same principles I had learned in that class (grammar, additional vocabulary, future and past tense, etc.) to those three hundred and fifty words I already had memorized, and immediately I felt as if I had grown wings and learned how to fly.

At the end of the semester, we took a class trip to San José, Costa Rica. I was like a fish in water, while the rest of my classmates were floundering and still struggling to converse. Throughout the following months, I again applied the same principle to other languages—French, Portuguese, Italian, and Arabic, all of which I now speak proficiently, thanks to this very simple technique.

This method is by far the fastest way to master quick and easy conversational language skills. There is no other technique that compares to my concept. It is effective, it worked for me, and it will work for you. Be consistent with my program, and you too will succeed the way I and many, many others have.

Contents

Introduction to the Program. 8

Memorization Made Easy. 10

The Emitari Dialect. 12

The Saudi Gulf Dialect. 45

The Qatari Dialect. 76

The Kuwaiti Dialect. 111

The Bahraini Dialect. 141

The Omani Dialect. 171

Conclusion 200

INTRODUCTION TO THE PROGRAM

People often dream about learning a foreign language, but usually they never do it. Some feel that they just won't be able to do it while others believe that they don't have the time. Whatever your reason is, it's time to set that aside. With my new method, you will have enough time, and you will not fail. You will actually learn how to speak the fundamentals of the language—fluently in as little as a few days. Of course, you won't speak perfect Saudi Gulf, Emirati, Qatari, Kuwaiti, Bahraini, and Omani Dialects at first, but you will certainly gain significant proficiency. For example, if you travel to the Gulf States, you will almost effortlessly be able engage in basic conversational communication with the locals in the present tense and you will no longer be intimidated by culture shock. It's time to relax. Learning a language is a valuable skill that connects people of multiple cultures around the world—and you now have the tools to join them.

How does my method work? I have taken twenty-seven of the most commonly used languages in the world and distilled from them the three hundred and fifty most frequently used words in any language. This process took three years of observation and research, and during that time, I determined which words I felt were most important for this method of basic conversational communication. In that time, I chose these words in such a way that they were structurally interrelated and that, when combined, form sentences. Thus, once you succeed in memorizing these words, you will be able to combine these words and form your own sentences. The words are spread over twenty pages. The words will also combine easily in sentences, for example, enabling you to ask simple questions, make basic statements, and obtain a rudimentary understanding of others' communications. I have also created Memorization Made Easy techniques for this program in order to help with the memorization of the vocabulary.

Introduction to the Program

Please also see Reading and Pronunciation of Arabic accents in order to gain proficiency in the reading and pronunciation of the Arabic language prior to starting this program. Please also see Reading and Pronunciation of Arabic accents in order to gain proficiency in the reading and pronunciation of the Arabic language prior to starting this program.

My book is mainly intended for basic present tense vocal communication, meaning anyone can easily use it to "get by" linguistically while visiting a foreign country without learning the entire language. With practice, you will be 100 percent understandable to native speakers, which is your aim. One disclaimer: this is not a grammar book, though it does address minute and essential grammar rules. Therefore, understanding complex sentences with obscure words in Arabic is beyond the scope of this book.

People who have tried this method have been successful, and by the time you finish this book, you will understand and be understood in basic conversational Arabic. This is the best basis to learn not only the Arabic language but any language. This is an entirely revolutionary, no-fail concept, and your ability to combine the pieces of the "language puzzle" together will come with great ease, especially if you use this program prior to beginning an Arabic class.

This is the best program that was ever designed to teach the reader how to become conversational. Other conversational programs will only teach you phrases. But this is the only program that will teach you how to create your own sentences for the purpose of becoming conversational.

MEMORIZATION MADE EASY

There is no doubt the three hundred and fifty words in my program are the required essentials in order to engage in quick and easy basic conversation in any foreign language. However, some people may experience difficulty in the memorization. For this reason, I created Memorization Made Easy. This memorization technique will make this program so simple and fun that it's unbelievable! I have spread the words over the following twenty pages. Each page contains a vocabulary table of ten to fifteen words. Below every vocabulary box, sentences are composed from the words on the page that you have just studied. This aids greatly in memorization. Once you succeed in memorizing the first page, then proceed to the second page. Upon completion of the second page, go back to the first and review. Then proceed to the third page. After memorizing the third, go back to the first and second and repeat. And so on. As you continue, begin to combine words and create your own sentences in your head. Every time you proceed to the following page, you will notice words from the previous pages will be present in those simple sentences as well, because repetition is one of the most crucial aspects in learning any foreign language. Upon completion of your twenty pages, congratulations, you have absorbed the required words and gained a basic, quick-and-easy proficiency and you should now be able to create your own sentences and say anything you wish in the **Najdi** Arabic dialect. This is a crash course in conversational Arabic, and it works!

Also by Yatir Nitzany

Conversational Spanish Quick and Easy

Conversational French Quick and Easy

Conversational Italian Quick and Easy

Conversational Portuguese Quick and Easy

Conversational German Quick and Easy

Conversational Russian Quick and Easy

Conversational Hebrew Quick and Easy

Conversational Yiddish Quick and Easy

Conversational Arabic Quick and Easy
Palestinian Arabic

Conversational Arabic Quick and Easy
Lebanese Dialect

Conversational Arabic Quick and Easy
Egyptian Dialect

Conversational Arabic Quick and Easy
Jordanian Dialect

Conversational
Arabic
Quick and Easy

EMIRATI ARABIC

YATIR NITZANY

THE EMIRATI DIALECT

Emirati Arabic is the main component of Gulf Arabic, which is a form of Arabic used in the United Arab Emirates (UAE), a country of around 9.5 million people. The UAE has borders with Oman and Saudi Arabia.

In the Northern Emirates, the dialect spoken is Shehhi, by the Al Shehhi people. Emirati or Gulf Arabic is often spoken in neighboring Gulf States, including Qatar, Kuwait, Bahrain, and Saudi Arabia. Shehhi Arabic is a less popular dialect spoken in the north of the country, but it is widely spoken in the neighboring state of Oman.

Locals use Emirati Arabic, while Modern Standard Arabic (MSA) holds higher prestige in schools and formal domains.

MSA is a modern form of Classical Arabic, with which the Qur'an was written, and is the official language of all Middle Eastern countries. It is an official means of communication, such as for the media and is not really used for social purposes. Any other version of Arabic is considered a dialect or referred to as colloquial Arabic. Most people in the Middle East and some parts of Africa speak some version of the language. Under most circumstances, they can use MSA to communicate with each other, despite their varying dialects. It is closely related to Islam, though many Muslims don't speak it.

The UAE has attracted large numbers of South Asian laborers over the past decades with around 85% of the population being expatriates. While there are different dialects spoken within the same country, there are many borrowed words, some mixed and some created from people and countries that were trade partners; for example, India, Africa, Portugal, Britain, and neighboring Arab countries. English is also widely spoken.

ARABIC PRONUNCIATIONS

PLEASE MASTER THE FOLLOWING PAGE IN ARABIC PRONUNCIATIONS PRIOR TO STARTING THE PROGRAM

Kha. For Middle Eastern languages including Arabic, Hebrew, Farsi, Pashto, Urdu, Hindi, etc., and also German, to properly pronounce the kh or ch is essential, for example, *Khaled* (a Muslim name) or *Chanukah* (a Jewish holiday) or *Nacht* ("night" in German). The best way to describe kh or ch is to say "ka" or "ha" while at the same time putting your tongue at the back of your throat and blowing air. It's pronounced similarly to the sound that you make when clearing your throat. Please remember this whenever you come across any word containing a *kh* in this program.

Ghayin. The Arabic *gh* is equivalent to the "g" in English, but its pronunciation more closely resembles the French "r," rather than "g." Pronounce it at the back of your throat. The sound is equivalent to what you would make when gargling water. Gha is pronounced more as "rha," rather than as "ga." *Ghada* is pronounced as "rhada." In this program, the symbol for *ghayin* is *gh*, so keep your eyes peeled.

Aayin is pronounced as a'a, pronounced deep at the back of your throat. Rather similar to the sound one would make when gagging. In the program, the symbol for *aayin* is a'a, u'u, o'o, or i'i.

Ha is pronounced as "ha." Pronunciation takes place deep at the back of your throat, and for correct pronunciation, one must constrict the back of the throat and exhale air while simultaneously saying "ha." In the program, this strong h ("*ha*") is emphasized whenever *ha, ah, hi, he,* or *hu* is encountered.

NOTE TO THE READER

The purpose of this book is merely to enable you to communicate in the Emirati Dialect. In the program itself (pages 17-39) you may notice that the composition of some of those sentences might sound rather clumsy. This is intentional. These sentences were formulated in a specific way to serve two purposes: to facilitate the easy memorization of the vocabulary and to teach you how to combine the words in order to form your own sentences for quick and easy communication, rather than making complete literal sense in the English language. So keep in mind that this is not a phrase book!

As the title suggests, the sole purpose of this program is for conversational use only. It is based on the mirror translation technique. These sentences, as well as the translations are not incorrect, just a little clumsy. Latin languages, Semitic languages, and Anglo-Germanic languages, as well as a few others, are compatible with the mirror translation technique.

Many users say that this method surpasses any other known language learning technique that is currently out there on the market. Just stick with the program and you will achieve wonders!

Note to the Reader

Again, I wish to stress this program is by no means, shape, or form a phrase book! The sole purpose of this book is to give you a fundamental platform to enable you to connect certain words to become conversational. Please also read the "Introduction" and the "About Me" section prior to commencing the program.

In order to succeed with my method, please start on the very first page of the program and fully master one page at a time prior to proceeding to the next. Otherwise, you will overwhelm yourself and fail. Please do not skip pages, nor start from the middle of the book.

It is a myth that certain people are born with the talent to learn a language, and this book disproves that myth. With this method, anyone can learn a foreign language as long as he or she follows these explicit directions:

* Memorize the vocabulary on each page

* Follow that memorization by using a notecard to cover the words you have just memorized and test yourself.

* Then read the sentences following that are created from the vocabulary bank that you just mastered.

* Once fully memorized, give yourself the green light to proceed to the next page.

Again, if you proceed to the following page without mastering the previous, you are guaranteed to gain nothing from this book. If you follow the prescribed steps, you will realize just how effective and simplistic this method is.

THE PROGRAM

Let's Begin! "Vocabulary"
(Memorize the Vocabulary)

I | I am	Ana
With you	Ma'ak / ma'ach
With him / with her	Ma'ah / ma'aha
With us	Ma'ana
For you	(Masc) lik / (Fem) lich
Without him	Min donah
Without them	Min donhom
Always	Doum
Was	Kan
This, This is	Hatha
Is, it's, it is	'Oho
Sometimes	Marrat
Maybe	Yimkin
Are you? / is it?	(M) int?(F) inti?/ 'oho?
Better	Ahsan
You, you are	(M)Inta / (F)inti
He / She	'Oho/'ehya
From	Min/Mni

Sentences from the vocabulary (now you can speak the sentences and connect the words)

I am with you
Ana ma'ak
This is for you
(M)Hatha lik/(F) Hatha lich
I am from UAE
Ana min elimarat
Are you from Iraq?
Int min el-Iraq?

Sometimes you are with us at the mall
Marrat int tkoon ma'ana fil mall
I am always with her
Ana dom ma'aha
Are you without them today?
Int min donhom elyom?
Sometimes I am with him
Marrat ana bakun ma'ah

*In Arabic, there are gender rules. Saying "for you" to a male is *lik*, but if you are talking to a female, then it's *lich*. In spoken Arabic, which has no rules, they say *Il kitab hatha lik*, but they also say *ilkitab hatha alashanik* or *ilkitab hatha lik*.
*In spoken Arabic, words like *hal* / "are" are usually dropped, and we only say *ehya aklat?*, *'oho Nayim?*, etc., which, if written in Classical Arabic, would have been *Hal aklat ehya?* / "has she eaten?" or *Hal 'oho Na'im?* / "has he slept?"

I was	Ana kint
To be	(M)Ykun/(F)Tkun
The	Il, el, al
Same / like *(as in similar)*	Mithl
Good	Zain
Here	Hnee
Very	Wayid
And	Ow
Between	Bain
Now	Elheen
Later / After / afterwards	Ba'dain
If	Law
Yes	Haih
To	Li
Tomorrow	Bachir
Person	WahId/ Shakhs
Also / too / as well	Ba'ad

If it was between now and later
Law chan bain elheen wo ba'dain
It's better tomorrow
Bachir ahsan
This is good as well
Hatha zain ba'ad
To be the same person
Ykun nafs ilshakhs
Yes, you are very good
Haih, inta wayid zain
I was here with them
Ana kint hnee ma'ahum
You and I
Inta w-ana
The same day
Nafs elyom

*In the Arabic language, adjectives follow the noun. For example, "the same day" is *nafs ilyom*, "small house" is *beit zigheer*, "tall person" is *wahid toweel*, and "short person" is *wahid giseer*.
*In this program the article "the" *(il, al)* will sometimes become a prefix at the beginning of the noun. For nouns beginning with *d, n, r, s, sh, t, th*, and *z*, the *l* is omitted and replaced with the initial consonant of the following noun. "The people" / *alshakhs* is *ishakhs*, "the Nile" / *il-nil is innil*. It is dropped when spoken; however, when written, it's usually *il-shaks* or *il-nil*.

The Program

Me	Ana, ni, li
Ok	Tayyib, zain
Even if	Hatta law
No	La
Worse	Akhas
Where	Wain
Everything	Kil shay
Somewhere	Mikan
What	Shoo?
Almost	No equivalent
There	Hnak
I go	Ana baseer

Afterwards is worse
Ba'dain ykun akhas
Even if I go now
Hatta law baseer elheen
Where is everything?
Wain kil shay?
Maybe somewhere
Yemkin fi ay mikan
Where are you?
Inta wain?

Fi mikan literally means in a place.
*In Arabic, the pronoun "me" has several definitions. In relation to verbs it's *ni* or *li*. Li refers to any verb that relates to the action of doing something to someone or for someone. For example, "tell me," "tell (to) me" / *khabrni*
Ni just means "me"; "love me" / *Hibbini*.
*"On me" / *Alay*, "in me" / *dakhli*
*"to me" / *li*, "With me" / *ma'ai*
*"in front of me" / *jeddami*, "from me" / *Minni*
The same rule applies for "him" and "her", both become suffixes; *'ohu* and *'ehya*;
*love her / *ahebha*, love him / *ahibbah*
*love them / *ahibum*, love us / *hibna*
Any verb that relates to doing something to someone, for someone put L
"Tell me" / *goolli*, *khabrni* "tell him" / *khabrah*,
"tell her" / *khabbirha*, "tell them"/ *khabbirhum*,
"tell us" / *khabbirna*.
Adding you as a suffix in Arabic is *ik* or *lak*. Female *ich* or *lich*
"Love you" / *ahibbik, ahibbich*, "tell you" / *Akhabrik* (F)*Akhabrich*.
*In Emirati Arabic there are a few ways of saying no, depending on where it falls in the sentence. You can say "*Ma shai faydih*" but you say, if asked something like, "are you going?" you would answer "*Laa*."

House	Bait
In, at, at the, in the	Fi/fi/fil /fil
Car	Motar
Already	Min zaman
Good morning	Sabah ilkhair
How are you?	Shakhbarik
Where are you from?	(M)Inta min wain?(F)Inti min wain?
Today	Elyom
Hello	Marhaba
What is your name?	(M)Shismik?/ (F)shismich?
How old are you?	Kam omrik?
Son	Wild
Daughter	Bint
To have	(M)Indah/(F)Indha
Doesn't / isn't	Ma / Mob
Hard	Sa'b
Still	Lilheen

She doesn't have a car, so maybe she is still at the house?
Hiyyi ma indha motar, 'alashan chi yemkin ehya lilheen belbait.
I am in the car already with your son and daughter
Ana bissayarah min ziman ma' wildik w-bintik
Good morning, how are you today?
Sabah al-khair, shakhbarik elyom?
Hello, what is your name?
Marhaba, shismik?
How old are you?
Kam omrak?
This is very hard, but it's not impossible
Hatha wayid sa'b, bas mob mustahil
Where are you from?
Inta min wain?

*In Emirati Arabic, possessive pronouns become suffixes to the noun. For example, in the translation for "your," *ak* is the masculine form, and *ich* is the feminine form.
* "your book" / *ktabak* (m.), *ktabich* (f.)
* "your house" / *baitak* (m.), *baitich* (f.)
*In the Arabic language, as well as in other Semitic languages, the article "a" doesn't exist. "She doesn't have a car" / *hiyyi ma indha sayyarah*.
*The definition of *khalas* can also be "done" or "finished."

The Program

Thank you	Shokran
For	Ala
Anything	Ay shay
That, That is	(M)Hathak/(F)Hathik
Time	Wa'gt
But	Bas
No/ Not	Laa/Mob
I am not	Ana mob/ma
Away	Bi'eed
Late	Mit'akkhir
Similar, like	Nafs/Mithl
Another/ Other	Ba'ad/Thani
Side	Soub/yam
Until	Lain
Yesterday	Ams
Without us	Min donna
Since	Min
Day	Yum
Before	Gabl

Thanks for anything
Shokran ala ay shay
It's already time
Ilwagt khallas min ziman
I am not here, I am away
Ana mo hnee, ana barrah
That is a similar house
Hatha nafs elbit
I am from the other side
Ana mni il-soub il thani
But I was here until late yesterday
Bas ana kint hnee lain ams
I am not at the other house
Ana mo filbait ilthani

*In Emirati Arabic there are 3 definitions for "time":
"Time", *wagt* refers to; era, moment period, duration of time.
"Time(s)", *marra(t)* refers to; occasion or frequency.
"Time", *sa'ah* in reference to; hour, what time is it?
Ayyi or *ayyu*, depending on where it falls in the sentence. This is the *ay*, in Classical Arabic, meaning "any". We stress the y, because this is how it is pronounced in Emirati.

I say / I am saying	Agool/atkallam
What time is it?	Kam Issa'ah?
I want	Ana aba
Without you	Min donik
Everywhere /wherever	Fi kil mikan/ Fi ay mikan
I am going	(M) Ana baseer/ barooh /(F) Ana baseer/ barooh
With	Ma'
My	mali
Cousin	(M) wild `ammi (or) Wild khali [uncle from mother's side), (P) 'iyal ammi /'iyal Khali (F)bint ammi/ bint khali, (P)banat ammi, banat khali
I need	Ana mihtaj
Right now	Alhaz/ alheen
Night	Lail
To see	Yshuf/ ytali'
Light	Lait
Outside	Barrah
Without	Min don
Happy	Mistanis
I see / I am seeing	Ana ashoof

I am saying no / I say no
Ana agul la'/ Ana agul la'
I want to see this today
Ana aba ashuf hatha elyom
I am with you everywhere
Ana ma'ak fi kil mikan
I am happy without my cousins here
Ana mistanis min don 'iyal 'ammi hnee
I need to be there at night
Ana mihtaj akun hnak fil-lail
I see light outside
Ana shayif lait barrah
What time is it right now?
Kam Issa'ah alheen

My,mali is also a possessive pronoun, mali means *my*, but also becomes a suffix to a noun.
For example; *cousins, 'iyal il'am / my cousin, Wild ammi or wild khali [maternal uncle's son] or Cup, glass/ my cup, glass mali.*
For second and third person masculine noun; *wild,son. Male; ik,ikum/ female; ich,ik um Your son; (M)wildik (F)wildich/ Your (plural) son; (M)wildkum (F)wildkum.* [In Emirati,
unlike Classical Arabic, plural female is not different from plural male] *His son; Wildah; Her son, Wildha. Our son, wildna / (M) and (F) Their son, wildhum.*
For second and third person we use feminine noun; *car, motarh Your car, sayyartik/ Your (plural) car; sayyaratkum /His car; sayyartah, Her car, sayyarat-ha, Our car, sayyaratna / (M) and (F)Their car, sayyarathum.*

Place	Mikan
Easy	Sahl, hayyin
To find	Yilga
To look for/to search	Ydawwir
Near / Close	Jireeb
To wait	Yitrayya
To sell	Yibee'
To use	Ystakhdim
To know	Yadri/ y'arif
To decide	Yqarrir
Between	Bain
Next to	Yam
To	Li

It's easy to find this place
Sahl telga Hatha Ilmikan
I want to look for this next to the car
Ana aba adawwir ala hatha end-ilmotar
I am saying to wait until tomorrow
Ana 'agool nantir lain bachir
This table is easy to sell
Hathi Il-tawlih sahla tinba'a
I want to use this
Ana aba ystakhdim hatha
I need to know the location of the house
Ana mihtaj a'arif mikan il-bait
I want to decide between both places
Ana aba aqarrir bain il mikanain

*Please pay close attention to the conjugation of verbs, whether they are in first person, second, or third. Unlike Anglo Germanic languages, Latin languages, or even Classical Arabic, in which the first verb is conjugated and the following is always infinitive, however in colloquial Arabic it is quite different. In Spoken Arabic, for example for first person tense, the first verb is conjugated into first person and the verb as well. For example: I need to know where is the house in Classical Arabic it will be *Innani bihajah (I need) ila ma'rifat* (to know [to know is infinitive) *makan al-manzil,* in Emirati Arabic it will be *Ana mihtaj (I need) a'araf* (the verb to know is conjugated into first person as well) *mikan il-bait.* The same rules apply to second as well as third person. Keep in mind the Emirati dialect of the Arabic language is considered a colloquial, rather than an official language.
*Mikan il-bait literally means the "location (or) place of the house."

Because	Ala sibbat
To buy	Yashtri
Life	Hayah/'umr
Them, They	Homma, Homma
Bottle	Gharshah
Book	Kitab
Mine	Mali
To understand	Yefham
Problem / Problems	Mishkelah/ Mishakel
I do / I am doing	'Asawwi
Of	Min
To look	Ytali'/ ynathir
Myself	'Umrii
Enough	Bas/ kafi
Food / water	Akl / Maay
Each/ every/ all /entire	Kil/ Kil/ kil/ kil
Hotel	Fundug'

I like this hotel because I want to look at the beach
Ana aheb hathal-Fundug' ala sibbat innah mgabel ala-shat
I want to buy a bottle of water
Ana aba ashri gharshat maay
I do this every day
Ana 'asawwi chi kil yom
Both of them have enough food
Humm ithninhum indhum akl kafi
That is the book, and that book is mine
Thak al-kitab, wthak al-kitab mali
I need to understand the problem
Ana mihtaj aftihim il-mishkilah
I see the view of the city from the hotel
Ana ashoof manthar il medeenah mnil-Findig
I do my homework today
Ana bassawil-wayib mali elyom
My entire life/ all my life
Kil Hayati/ Kil Hayati

*"Bottle of water" / *gharshat maay* (The use of "of" isn't always required in Arabic.)
**Chi* means "like this" or "this way."
*The definition of *mgabel* is "to look at."

The Program

I like	Ana 'ahib
There is / There are	Fi
Family / Parents	'Aylah, hal/ oboy w-ommi
Why	Laish
To say	Ygooll, yitkallam
Something	Shay
To go	Yruh/ yseer
Ready	Zahib
Soon	Greeb
To work	'Ashtighil
Who	Minou
Busy	Mashgul
That (conjunction)	Elli, ennah
I Must	Ana lazim
Important	Muhim

I like to be at my house with my parents
Ana 'ahib akun fi baiti ma' oboy w-ommy
I want to know why I need to say something important
Ana aba a'arif laish lazim 'agool shay muhim
I am there with her
Ana hnak ma'aha
I am busy, but I need to be ready soon
Ana mashghul, bas ana mihtaj azhab greeb
I like to go to work
Ana 'ahib aruh ishshughil
Who is there?
Minou hnak?
I want to know if they are here, because I want to go outside
Ana aba a'arif itha hum hnee, alashan ana aba ath-har' barra
There are seven dolls
Fi sab' al'ab
I need to know that that is a good idea
Ana mihtaj a'arif inna hathi fikrah zainah

*In the last sentence we use "that" as a conjunction *(inna/inni)* and as a demonstrative pronoun *(hatha/hathi)*. *Bsir'ah* literally means "quickly."
**Mawjud* literally means "exist," but it also means "there is" or "there are" or "present."
*In Emirati Arabic, "to go" is *yruh / yseer*; however, *"to go out"* is *ath-har*.

How much /How many	Ish gad? Kam? Cham?
To bring	Yiyeeb
With me	Ma'ai
Instead	Badal
Only	Bas
When	Mita/ min
I can / Can I?	Ana 'aroum/ Ana 'aroum?
Or	Walla/aw
Were	Kan/ chan
Without me	Min dony
Fast	Siree'
Slow	Biteei'
Cold	Barid
Inside	Dakhil
To eat	Yakil
Hot	Haar
To Drive	Ysoog

How much money do I need to bring with me?
Cham Ana mihtaj ayeeb bizat ma'ai?
Instead of this cake, I want that cake
Badal hathi elkekah, aba theech elkekah
Only when you can
Bas min troum
They were without me yesterday
Chanu min doni ams
Do I need to drive the car fast or slow?
Ana mihtaj asoog il-motar bsir'ah aw bitee'?
It is cold inside the library
Il jaw barid dakhil il-maktabah
Yes, I like to eat this hot for my lunch
Heih, ana 'aheb akil il-'akl haar chi
I can work today
Ana aroum ashtighil elyom

*"Were / *kan* or *chan*, but for "they were," add the suffix to the pronoun: *kanu* or *chanu*. "We were" is *kinna* or *chinna*.
*In Emirati Arabic, *il jaw* means "the climate, weather, temperature, etc."
Chi literally means "this way." However, when we say, *haar chi*, we are saying, "this hot."
*In Emirati Arabic, *ish-gad bizat* literally translated means "how much money."
*In Emirati Arabic, "money" can be either *bizat* or *floos*.

The Program

To answer	Yrid
To fly	Ytir
Time / Times	Wagt/Marrah, Awgat/Marrat
To travel	Ysafir
To learn	Yiti'allam
How	Kaif
To swim	Yasbah
To practice	Ytdarab
To play	Yal'ab
To leave (something)	Ykhalli
Many /much /a lot	Wayid
I go to	Ana baseer il
First	Awwal
World	Alam
Around	Jereeb il

I want to answer many questions
Ana aba arid ala wayid as'ilah
I must travel to Dubai today
Ana Lazim asafir Dubai elyom
I need to learn how to swim at the pool
Ana mihtaj ati'allam issibaha fi elmasbah
I want to learn to play better tennis
Ana aba ati'allam li'b il tennis zain
I want to leave this here for you when I go to travel the world
Ana aba akhalli hatha hnee 'alashanak, min asafir walif ilAlam
Since the first time
Min awwal marrah
The children are yours
Thola 'iyalik

*In Emirati Arabic; to leave (something) is *yrooh*. To leave (a place) is *akhalli il mikan*.
*In Emirati Arabic there are 3 definitions for time:
"Time", *wagt* refers to; era, moment period, duration of time.
"Time(s)", *marra(t)* refers to; occasion or frequency.
"Time", *sa'ah* in reference to; hour, what time is it.
**Thola* literally means "those," but again, when we want to say, "the children are yours" in Emirati, we do say, *thola 'iyalik*, meaning, "the children in question" or "the children referred to."
*The definition of *walif* is "to go around."
*With the knowledge you've gained so far, now try to create your own sentences!

Nobody / Anyone	Ma-had/ay wahid
Against	A'ks
Us	Hinna
To visit	Yzur
Mom / Mother	'Ummi
To give	Ya'ati
Which	Ay
To meet	Yiltigi
Someone	Wahid
Just	Bas
To walk	Yamshi
Week	Usbu'
Towards	Saob
Than	Min
Nothing	Ma shay

Something is better than nothing
Shay ahsan min ma shay
I am against her
Ana a'ks-ha
We go to visit my family each week
Hinna binruh bait hali kil usbu'u
I need to give you something
Ana mihtaj a'ateek shay
Do you want to go meet someone?
Tiba truh tiltigi wahid?
I was here on Wednesdays as well
Ana kint hnee al-arba' ba'ad
Do you do this everyday?
Inta tsawwi chi kil yum?
You need to walk, but not towards the house
Inta mihtaj titimasha, bas mob saob il-bait

*In Emirati Arabic when using the pronoun you as a direct and indirect object pronoun (the person who is actually affected by the action being carried out) in relation to a verb, the pronoun, you, becomes a suffix to that verb. That suffix becomes (Masc)*ik* (Fem)*ich*.
To give, *yinti* / to give you, *yinteek* To tell, *ygul*/ to tell you, (M)*ygullik* (F)*ygullich*.
See you, *ashufik* /to see you (Plural), (M) *ashufkum*, (F) *ashufkum* [in Emirati they address males and females the same]
For third person male add "u" (plural)humma and for female add "hin":(plural) hum.
Tell him *Agullah* / tell her, *Agullha* / see them, (M)*ashufhum* (F)*ashufhum* / see us, *Shufna*.
*The definition of *sawwi chi* is "do this" or "do it like this".
Tiba signifies "you want."

The Program

I have	Ana Indi
Don't	Ma
Friend	Ribee'
To borrow	Yigtirith/ yisti'eer
To look like / resemble	Yishbah
Grandfather	Yad
To want	Aba
To stay	Ytam
To continue	Ykammil
Way (road, path)	Tireej/share'
Way (method)	Tiriga
I dont	Ana ma
To show	Yrawi
To prepare	Yzahhib
I am not going	Ana mob rayeh

Do you want to look like Salim
Inta tiba tishbih Salim?
I want to borrow this book for my grandfather
Ana aba asti'ir hatha ilkitab hag yaddi
I want to drive and to continue on this way to my house
Ana aba asug wa-kammil ala hatha il-tireej lain baiti
This isn't the way to do this
Hathi mihi-ttiriga alashan nsawwi hath ishay?
I have a friend there, that's why I want to stay in Abu Dhabi
Ana indi rifeej hnak, alashan chi aba atam fi-Abu Dhabi
I am not going to see anyone here
Ana mob rayih ashuf ay wahid hnee
I need to show you how to prepare breakfast
Ana mihtaj araweek kaif tzahhib il-ryoog
Why don't you have the book?
Laish ma indik il-kitab?
That is incorrect, I don't need the car today
Hatha mob sidj, ana mob mihtaj il-motar elyom

Sidj means "correct"; however, mob *sidj* means "incorrect."
Indik means "to have." "I have" is *ana indi*; however, "I don't have" is *Ana ma indi*.
Lain means "up to" or "to" as the final destination. It basically signifies "until."
*In Emirati Arabic, "to want" is *yiba*, "I want" is *aba*, "he wants" is *yiba*, and "she wants" is *tiba*.
*"Friend" is *rifeej*; however, the masculine and feminine forms are *rifeeji* (m.) and *rifeejtiti* (f.).
Hag indicates possession, such as "for/to."
Hatha + il + shay merged to be hath-ishay.

To remember	Yathkir
Your	Lik
Number	Ragam
Hour	Sa'ah
Dark / darkness	Thalmah
About / on the	'An / 'al al
Grandmother	yaddah
Five	Khamsah
Minute / Minutes	Digigah
More	Zyada
To think	Yfakkir
To do	Asawwi
To come	Yiji/ayee
To hear	Yasma'
Last	Akhir
To talk / To Speak	Ygool/ yitkallam

You need to remember my number
Inta mihtaj tathkir ragami
This is the last hour of darkness
hathi akhir sa'a min il-thalmah
I want to come to hear my grandmother speak Arabic
Ana aba ayee asma' yadditi titkallam Arabi
I need to think more about this, and what to do
Ana mihtaj afakkir zyada fi-hatha-lmawthoo', wshassawi
From here to there, it's only five minutes
min hnee lain hnak khams digayig bas
The school on the mountain
Il madrasah ala al-jabal

*Lmawthoo' literally means "topic," "subject."
*Wsh (what) + assawi (to do).

The Program

Early	Taw elnas
To leave (to go)	Yrooh
Again	Marrah thanyah
Arabic	Arabi
To take	Yakhith
To try	Yjarrib
To rent	Yesta'jir
Without her	Min donha
We are	Hinna
To turn off	Ybannid
To ask	Yes'al
To stop	Yogaf
Permission	Rikhsah
While	(no equivalent)

He needs to leave and rent a house at the beach
'Iho mihtaj yrooh w-yisti'jir bait ala al bahar
I want to take the test without her
Ana aba akhith il'imtihan min-donha
We are here a long while
Hinna binkoon hnee wayid wagt
I need to turn off the lights tonight
Ana mihtaj abannid illait illailah
We want to stop here
Hinna niba nogaf hnee
We are from Dubai
Hinna mni-dbai
The same building
Nafs Il-binayah
I want to ask permission to leave
Ana aba atlub rikhsah 'alashan arooh

*In Emirati Arabic, *b-intam* gives the meaning that we have been and will continue to be here for a long while. *B-intam*, literally speaking, means "will stay."
*In Arabic, *alashan* means "because," but its usage can also mean "to" and "in order to."

To open	Ybattil
A bit, a little, a little bit	Shway
To pay	Yadfa'
Once again	Ba'id Marrah/marrah thanyah
There isn't/ there aren't	Ma shay
Sister	'Ikht
To hope	Yitimanna
To live (to exist)	Yi'ish
To live (in a place)	Yaskin
Nice to meet you	Hayyak allah
Name	Ism
Last name	Ism il 'aylah
To return	Raj'ah / y'awid/ yrid
Sad	Za'lan
Door	Bab/bawwabah

I need to open the door for my sister
Ana mihtaj abattil il-bab hagg-ikhti

I need to buy something
Ana Mihtaj ashri shay

I want to meet your sisters
Aba altigi ikhtik

Nice to meet you, what is your name and your last name
Hayyak allah, shismik wshism il'aylah maltik?

To hope for a little better
Yitimanna shay ahsan

I want to return to Qatar
Ana aba Arid gitar

I want to live 100 years
Ana aba a'ish 'imyat sanah

I need to return your book
Ana mihtaj aridlik il-kitab

Why are you sad right now?
(M)laish inta za'lan elheen'? (F) laish inti za'lanah elheen?

There aren't any people here
Ma shay nas hnee

There isn't enough time to go to Burj Dubai today
Ma shay wagt alashan nrooh-Bruj Dubai elyom

To happen	Yseer
To order	Yatlib/y'amir/ywassi
To drink	Yashrab
Excuse me	Min rikhistik/ issimohah
Child	(M)yahil (F)bint
Woman	Hirmah
To begin / To start	Yabda'
To finish	Yikhallas
To help	Ysa'id
To smoke	Ydookh
To love	Yhib
Afternoon	Elthuher

This must happen today
Hatha lazim yseer elyom
Excuse me, my child is here with me as well
Issimohah, wildi ba'ad ma'ai hnee
I love you
Ahibbik
I see you
Ana shayfik
I need you at my side
Ana mihtajak yammi
I need to begin soon in order to be able to finish before 3 o'clock in the afternoon
Ana mihtaj abda' bsir'ah alashan akhallis gabl issa'ah thalathah elthuher
I need help
Ana mihtaj msa'adah
I don't want to smoke once again
Ana maba adookh marrah thanyah
I want to learn how to speak Arabic
Ana aba ati'allam kaif atikallam 'Arabi

*"To help" is *ysa'id*. However, "help!" is *msa'adah*.
"I need help" or "I need rescue" / *ana mihtaj msa'adih*.
*The definition of *alashan* is "in order to."

To read	Yagra'
To write	Yaktib
To teach	Ydarris/ y'allim
To close	Ybannid
To choose	Yikhtar/ ynagg'i
To prefer	Yfathil
To put	Ykhalli
Less	Agal
Sun	Shams
Month	Shahr
I Talk	Ana agool/atikallam
Exact	Bithabt/ 'adil

I need this book in order to learn how to read and write in the Arabic language because I want to study in the UAE
Ana mihtaj hatha il-kitab 'alashan ati'allam il-grayah wilkitabah billughah il-arabiiyyah alashan adris fi-il Imarat
I want to close the door of the house
Ana aba abannid bab al-bait
I prefer to put the gift here
Ana afathil akhalli il-hidiyyah hnee
I want to pay less than you for the dinner
Ana aba adfa' agal minnik ala il-'asha
I speak with the boy and the girl in French
Ana batkallam ma'a ilwalad wilbint bil faransi
There is sun outside today
Il-shams tal'ah barrah elyom
Is it possible to know the exact date?
Mumkin n'arif il-tarikh bithabt?
I want to sleep
Ana aba nam
Where is the airport
Wain il-matar

To exchange (*money*)	Sarf/tabdil floos
To call	Yittisil
Brother	Akh
Dad	Oboy
To sit	Yilis
Together	Ma'a ba'th/ siwa
To change	Yghayyir/yitghayyar
Of course/certainly	Tab'an / akeed
Welcome	Hala/marhaba
During	no equivalent
Years	Sneen
Sky	Sama
Up	Fu'g
Down	Taht
Sorry	Asif/ assomohah
To follow	Yilhag
To the	Lil/ Ala-l
Big	Kibeer
New	Yideed
Never / ever	Abad

I don't want to exchange this money at the bank
Ana ma aba abaddil ilfloos fil bank
I want to call my brother and my son today
Ana aba attisil hag-okhuy wwildi elyom
Of course I can come to the theater, and I want to sit together with you and with your sister
Akid aroum ayee al-masrah, w-aba aylis ma'ak w-ma'a ikhtik
I need to go down to see your new house
Ana mihtaj anzil alashan ashuf baitik il-yideed
I can see the sky from the window
Ana aroum ashuf issima min al-direeshah
I am sorry, but he wants to follow her to the store
Ana assif, bas huwwa yiba yilhagha ala-l-mahal
I don't ever want to see you
Ana ma aba ashufik abad

*In Emirati Arabic, "brother" is *akh*, and "dad" is *ab*. However, "my dad" is oboy, and "my brother" is okhuy. "My sister" is ikhti, and "my mother" is ommi.
*In the English language, the verb "to go down" isn't commonly used. However, in many foreign languages, the use of this verb is quite prevalent.

To allow	Yasmah
To believe	Ysaddig/y'amin
Morning	Sobah
Except	Illa
To promise	Yew'id
Good night	Tisbah ala khair
To recognize	Yit'arraf
People	Ahal, nas, awadim
To move (an object)	Yharrik
To move (to a place)	Yintigil
Far	Bi'eed
Different	Gher
Man	Rayyal
To enter	Yadkhil
To receive	Yistilim
Pleasant	Tayeeb / hleelah
Good afternoon	Masa'a-il-Khair
Left / right	Yisar, Yimeen
Him / Her	Luh/ laha

I need to allow him to go with us, because he is a different person now
Ana mihtaj asmahlah yee ma'ana, ala sibbat ennah tighayyar alheen w-sar wahid gher
I believe everything except this
Ana asaddig kil shay illa hatha
I need to move the car because my sister needs to return home
Ana mihtaj aharrik il-motar ala sebbat enni-khti mihtajah trid il-bait
I promise to say good night to my parents each night
Wa'd inni amassi ala ommy woboy kil lailah
The people from UAE are very pleasant
Il-Imaratiyyin taybeen wayid
I need to find another hotel very quickly
Ana mihtaj alagi findig thani bsir'ah hail
They need to receive a book for work
Humma mihtajin yistilmun kitab hagg ishighil
I see the sun in the morning
Ana ashuf ilshams fissubah
The house is on the right side of the street
Il-bait mawjud ala ilsaob il-yimeen mni-shari'

*In Arabic, the article "the" is used when referring to countries, cities, or locations. "From UAE" / *min il Imarat.*
*Enni signifies first person possession: *Enni* (my) + *khti* (sister).

The Program

To wish	Yitimanna
Bad	Sayyi'
To Get	Yeeb/ yakhith
To forget	Yansa
Although	(no equivalent)
Everybody / Everyone	Kil wahid/ il-kil
To feel	Yhis
Past	Zaman
Next (following, after)	'Alhath / ilmarrah-ilyaya
To like	Yi'jib/ yhib
In front	Jiddam
Next (near, close)	Jireeb / yam
Behind	Wara
Well (as in doing well)	'Adil
Goodbye	Ma' issalamah
Restaurant	Mat'am
Bathroom	Hammam

I don't want to wish you anything bad
Ana ma aba atimannalik ayy shay sayyi'
I must forget everybody from my past in order to feel well
Ana lazim ansa kil illi kanu fi hayati ziman 'alashan aseer zein
I am next to the person behind you
Ana yam-ilshakhs illi warak
There is a great person in front of me
Fi shakhs zain jiddami
Goodbye my friends
Ma' issalamah ya rab'i
Where is the bathroom in the restaurant?
Wain Il-hamman illi fil-mat'am?
She has to buy a car before the next year
ehi lazim tishtiri motar gabl il-sanah ilyayah
I like the house, but it is very small
Il-bait ayibni, bas huwwa wayid sigheer

*In Emirati Arabic, *aseer* means "to be" or "to become."

To remove / to take out	Yishil
Please	Min fathlik/law simaht/isomohah
Beautiful	(M)helo, (F) helweh
To lift	Yirfa'a
Correct	Sah
Belong	Mal'
To hold	Yalgif/ ytam/ ykhalli
To check	Yifhas
Small	Sigheer
Real	Sidj
Weather	Ijjaw
Size	Hajm/ gyas/ kubr/ misahah
High	'Ali
Doesn't	Ma
So (as in then)	'Alashan chi/ ya'ni
So (as in very)	Wayid
Price	Si'ir/ thiman
Diamond	Almas

She wants to remove this door please
Ehya tiba tshil hatha-lbab min fathlik
This week the weather was very beautiful
Il-usbu' hatha, il jaw chan wayid hilo
I need to know which is the real diamond
Ana mihtaj a'arif ayya wihdah fihum hiyya il al-masah il-sidj
We need to know the size of the house
Ihna mihtajin n'arif kubr il-bait
I want to lift this, so you need to hold it high
Ana aba arfa'a hatha, alashan chi int mihtaj tkhalleh 'ali
I can pay this even though that the price is so expensive
Ana 'arum adfa'a hatha hata law chan il-mablagh hatta wayid ghali
Including everything, is this price correct?
Itha hasabna kil shay, hatha il-ssi'ir bekon 'adil?

*In Arabic, the articles "this" and "that" become reversed when preceding a noun. "This" (*hatha*) "week" (*usbu'*) becomes *hatha il-'usbu'*.
*In Emirati Arabic, *il-mablagh* means "the amount."

BUILDING BRIDGES

In Building Bridges, we take six conjugated verbs that have been selected after studies I have conducted for several months in order to determine which verbs are most commonly conjugated into first person. For example, once you know how to say, "I need," "I want," "I can," and "I like," you will be able to connect words and say almost anything you want more correctly and understandably. The following three pages contain these six conjugated verbs in first, second, third, fourth, and fifth person, as well as some sample sentences. Please master the entire program up until here prior to venturing onto this section.

I want	Ana aba
I need	Ana mihtaj
I can	Ana 'arum
I like	Ana ahib/ yi'jibni
I go	Ana aruh/aseer
I have	Ana indi
I must / I have to	Ana lazim, wajib alay

I want to go to my house
Ana aba aruh baiti
I can go with you to the bus station
Ana 'arum aruh ma'ak ala mujamma' il-basat
I need to walk to the museum
Ana mihtaj amshi lain il-mat-haf
I like to ride the train Ana ahib arkab il-qitar
I have to speak to my teacher
Ana lazim 'atkallam ma' il-mudarris haggi
I have a book
Ana indi kitab

Please master pages #17-#39, prior to attempting the following pages!!

You want / do you want - Inta tiba/ Inta tiba?
He wants / does he want - howwa yiba/ howwa yiba?
She wants / does she want - ehya tiba/ ehya tiba?
We want / do we want - hinna niba/ hinna niba?
They want / do they want – homma yibon/ homma yibon?
You (plural) want / - Intom tabon/ Intom tabon?

You need / do you need - Inta mihtaj/ inta mihtaj?
He needs / does he need – Howwa mihtaj/ howwa mihtaj?
She needs / does she need - ehya mihtajah/ ehya mihtajah?
We need / do we need - hinna mihtajin/ hinna mihtajin?
They need / do they need - homma mihtajin/ homma mihtajin?
You (plural) need/ do you need? - intom mihtajin/ intom Mihtajin?

You can / can you - Inta trum/ Inta trum?
He can / can he - Howwa yrum/ howwa yrum?
She can / can she - ehya trum/ ehya trum?
We can / can we - hinna nrum/ hinna nrum?
They can / can they - homma yrumon/ homma yrumon?
You (plural) can - intom trumon/ intom trumon?

You like / do you like – Inta t'hib/ Inta t'hib?
He likes / does he like – Howwa yhib/ howwa yhib?
She like / does she like – ehya thib/ ehya thib?
We like / do we like – hinna nhib/ hinna nhib?
They like / do they like - homma yhibbon/ homma yhibbon?
You (plural) like – intom t-hibbon/ intom t-hibbon?

You go / do you go - Inta troh/ Inta troh?
He goes / does he go - Howwa yroh/ howwa yruoh?
She goes / does she go - ehya trum/ ehya trum?
We go / do we go - hinna nroh/ hinna nroh?
They go / do they go – homma yrohon/ homma yrohon?
You (plural) go/ do you go – intom trohon/ intom trohon?

You have / do you have – Int indik/ Int indik?
He has / does he have – Howwa indah/ howwa indah?
She has / does she have – ehya indha/ ehya indha?
We have / do we have – hinna indna/ hinna indna?
They have / do they have – homma indhom/ homma indhom?
You (plural) have/ do you have – intom indkom/ intom indkom?

You must /must you? – Inta lazim/ Inta lazim?
He must/ must he? – Howwa lazim/ Howwa lazim?
She must/ must she – ehya lazim/ ehya lazim?
We must/ must we? - hinna lazim/ hinna lazim?
They must / must they? – homma lazim/ homma lazim?
You (plural) must/ must you? – intom lazim/ intom lazim?

Please master pages #17-#39, prior to attempting the following!!

Do you want to go?
Inta tiba truh?
Does he want to fly?
Huwwa yiba ytir?
We want to swim
Hinna niba nisbah
Do they want to run?
Humma yiboon yirkuthoon?
Do you need to clean?
Inta mihtaj tnathif?
She needs to sing a song
ehya mihtajah tghanni ughniyih
We need to travel
hinna mihtajin nsafir
They don't need to fight
Humma mob mihtajin yit-thrabon
You (plural) need to see
Intum mihtajin tshufun
Can you hear me?
Inta trum tisma'ni?
Yes, he can dance very well
haih, huwwa yrum yurgis wayid hilo
We can go out tonight
hinna nrum nith-har il-lailah
They can break the wood
Humma yrumon ykasrun il-hatab
Do you like to eat here?
Inta t-hib takil hnee?
He likes to spend time here
Huwwa yhib ygathi alwagt hnee
We like to fix the house
hinna nhib nsallih il-bait
They like to cook
Humma yhibbon al-tabkh
You (plural) like my house
intum t-hibbon baiti
Do you go to school today?
Inta rayih il-madrasah-lyom?
He goes fishing
Huwwa rayih yseed simach
We are going to relax
hinna rayhin nistanis
They go to watch a film
Humma rayhin yihthoron film
Do you have money?
Int indik bizat/ floos?
She must look outside
Hiyya Lazim ittali' barra
We have to sign our names
hinna lazim nwaggi' asfal asamina
They have to send the letter
Humma lazim ywaddon il-risalah
You (plural) have to order
Antum lazim twassun/ ttlboon

Countries of the Middle East
Dowal il-sharq il-awsat

Lebanon	Libnan
Syria	Surya
Jordan	Il-irdin
Israel/Palestine/West Bank	Isra'il/Falastin/il-thiffih il-gharbiyyih
Iraq	Il-Iraq
Saudi Arabia	Il-Su'udiyyih
Kuwait	Il-Kuwait
Qatar	Qitar
Bahrain	Il-Bahrain
United Arab Emirates	Il-Imarat
Oman	Uman
Yemen	Yaman
Egypt	Masir
Libya	Libya
Tunisia	Tunis
Algeria	Il-jazaier
Morocco	Il-Maghrib

Months

January	Kanun il-thani /yanayer
February	Shbat / febrayer
March	Athar /mars
April	Nisan / abriel
May	Ayyar / mayo
June	Huzayran / yonyo
July	Tammuz / yolyo
August	Aab/ agustus
September	Aylul / sebtember
October	Tishreen awwal / october
November	Tishreen thani / nofember
December	Kanun awwal / december

Days of the Week

Sunday	Yum il-ahad
Monday	Yum il-ithnin
Tuesday	Yum il-thulatha'
Wednesday	Yum al-'arbi'aa
Thursday	Yum il-khamees
Friday	Yum il-jom'a
Saturday	Yum issabt

Seasons

Spring	Rabee'
Summer	Saif
Autumn	Khareef
Winter	Ishta

Cardinal Directions

North	Shimal
South	Yanoob
East	Sharg
West	Gharb

Colors

Black	(M)Aswad (F)Suda
White	(M)Abyath (F)Baitha
Gray	(M)Ramadi (F)Ramadiyyih
Red	(M)Ahmar (F)Hamra
Blue	(M)Azrag(F)Zarga
Yellow	(M)Asfar (F)Safra
Green	(M)Akhthar (F)Khathra
Orange	(M)Burtuqali/(F)Burtuqaliyyih
Purple	(M)Banafsaji/(F)Banafsajia
Brown	(M)Binni (F)Binniyyah

Numbers

One	Wahid
Two	Ithnain
Three	Thalathah
Four	Arba'
Five	Khams
Six	Sittah
Seven	Sab'
Eight	Timanyah
Nine	Tis'
Ten	'Ashr

Twenty	'Ishreen
Thirty	Thalatheen
Forty	Arb'een
Fifty	Khamseen
Sixty	Sitteen
Seventy	Sab'een
Eighty	Thimaneen
Ninety	Tis'een
Hundred	Emyah
Thousand	Alf
Million	Milyun

Conversational Arabic Quick and easy

SAUDI GULF DIALECT

YATIR NITZANY

THE SAUDI GULF DIALECT

The population of Saudi Arabia is estimated at 33 million people. As with other Arabic countries, Modern Standard Arabic is the standard national language spoken by all. It is a formal language mainly used for government communications and media.

The main languages spoken in the country are Gulf Arabic, the Najdi dialect, and Hijazi.

Although spoken over much of Saudi Arabia's area, Gulf Arabic is not the native tongue of most Saudis. There are some 500,000 Gulf Arabic speakers in the country and they reside mostly in the Eastern Province. There are approximately 8.8 million Gulf Arabic speakers worldwide.

The most populous province, and the largest by area, is the Eastern Province, which is also home to most of Saudi Arabia's oil production and to a global hub for chemical industries. Because of its link with the oil-producing region in Saudi Arabia and the English-speaking oil-production companies and history of the area, there are many English loan words in the language.

Its location on the coast of the Persian Gulf also makes the Eastern Province a tourist area as well. Its capital is the city of Dammam, where most of the region's population live and where the seat of government is hosted. The Eastern Province is the third most populous province in the country, after Makkah and Riyadh. Dammam is the sixth most populous city in the whole of Saudi Arabia.

The remaining Arabic speakers in the province speak one of the other two dialects, more commonly the Najdi dialect.

While Gulf Arabic is mainly spoken by people living in Kuwait, Qatar, and the United Arab Emirates, it is also spoken by a minority of the population of Saudi Arabia and Bahrain, as well as a small pocket of the population of Iraq. Approximately one-third of the population of Oman speaks the Gulf Arabic dialect.

ARABIC PRONUNCIATIONS

PLEASE MASTER THE FOLLOWING PAGE IN ARABIC PRONUNCIATIONS PRIOR TO STARTING THE PROGRAM

Kha. For Middle Eastern languages including Arabic, Hebrew, Farsi, Pashto, Urdu, Hindi, etc., and also German, to properly pronounce the kh or ch is essential, for example, *Khaled* (a Muslim name) or *Chanukah* (a Jewish holiday) or *Nacht* ("night" in German). The best way to describe kh or ch is to say "ka" or "ha" while at the same time putting your tongue at the back of your throat and blowing air. It's pronounced similarly to the sound that you make when clearing your throat. Please remember this whenever you come across any word containing a kh in this program.

Ghayin. The Arabic gh is equivalent to the "g" in English, but its pronunciation more closely resembles the French "r," rather than "g." Pronounce it at the back of your throat. The sound is equivalent to what you would make when gargling water. Gha is pronounced more as "rha," rather than as "ga." *Ghada* is pronounced as "rhada." In this program, the symbol for *ghayin* is gh, so keep your eyes peeled.

Aayin is pronounced as a'a, pronounced deep at the back of your throat. Rather similar to the sound one would make when gagging. In the program, the symbol for *aayin* is a'a, u'u, o'o, or i'i.

Ha is pronounced as "ha." Pronunciation takes place deep at the back of your throat, and for correct pronunciation, one must constrict the back of the throat and exhale air while simultaneously saying "ha." In the program, this strong h ("ha") is emphasized whenever *ha, ah, hi, he,* or *hu* is encountered.

NOTE TO THE READER

The purpose of this book is merely to enable you to communicate in the Saudi Gulf Arabic dialect. In the program itself (pages 17-38) you may notice that the composition of some of those sentences might sound rather clumsy. This is intentional. These sentences were formulated in a specific way to serve two purposes: to facilitate the easy memorization of the vocabulary and to teach you how to combine the words in order to form your own sentences for quick and easy communication, rather than making complete literal sense in the English language. So keep in mind that this is not a phrase book!

As the title suggests, the sole purpose of this program is for conversational use only. It is based on the mirror translation technique. These sentences, as well as the translations are not incorrect, just a little clumsy. Latin languages, Semitic languages, and Anglo-Germanic languages, as well as a few others, are compatible with the mirror translation technique.

Many users say that this method surpasses any other known language learning technique that is currently out there on the market. Just stick with the program and you will achieve wonders!

Note to the Reader

Again, I wish to stress this program is by no means, shape, or form a phrase book! The sole purpose of this book is to give you a fundamental platform to enable you to connect certain words to become conversational. Please also read the "Introduction" and the "About Me" section prior to commencing the program.

In order to succeed with my method, please start on the very first page of the program and fully master one page at a time prior to proceeding to the next. Otherwise, you will overwhelm yourself and fail. Please do not skip pages, nor start from the middle of the book.

It is a myth that certain people are born with the talent to learn a language, and this book disproves that myth. With this method, anyone can learn a foreign language as long as he or she follows these explicit directions:

* Memorize the vocabulary on each page

* Follow that memorization by using a notecard to cover the words you have just memorized and test yourself.

* Then read the sentences following that are created from the vocabulary bank that you just mastered.

* Once fully memorized, give yourself the green light to proceed to the next page.

Again, if you proceed to the following page without mastering the previous, you are guaranteed to gain nothing from this book. If you follow the prescribed steps, you will realize just how effective and simplistic this method is.

The Program

Let's Begin! "Vocabulary" (Memorize the Vocabulary)

I | I am - Ana
With you – (M) ana ma'ak / (F) ana ma'ach
With him / with her - Ma'aah / Ma'aha
With us - Ma'ana
For you - (**Masc**) 'Ashanak / (**Fem**) Ashanech
Without him - Bedonah
Without them - Bedonhom
Always – Dayman
Was – Kan
This, this is, it's, it is – (**M**) Hatha, Hatha ho (**F**) Hathy, Hathy hey
Sometimes – Ahyanan
Maybe – Yemkin
You / you are / are you – (M) Ent (F) Enty
You (plural) - Entoum
Is it - (M) Wesh ho, (F) Wesh hey
Today – Alyom
Better – Ahsan
He / he is - Ho
She / she is - He
From - Min

This is for you
(M) Hatha ashank (F) Hatha ashanech **I am from Saudi**
Ana min al saudia
Are you from Riyadh?
Int min el-Riyadh?
I am with you
(M) Ana ma'ak (F) Ana ma'ach
Sometimes you are with us at the mall
(M) Ahyanan int ma'ana fel mall
(F) Ahyanan enty ma'ana fel mall
I am always with her
Ana dayman ma'aha
Are you without them today?
Ent bdonhom alyoum?
Sometimes I am with him
Ahyanan ana ma'ah

*In Saudi Gulf Arabic, with the question "is it?", the "it" can pertain to either a masculine or feminine noun. However, whenever pertaining to a masculine or feminine noun, it will become *ho* or *he*. For example, when referring to a feminine noun such as *sayaara* ("the car), "is it (the car in question) here?" / *he hena*? When referring to a masculine noun such as *kalb* ("a dog), "is it (the dog in question) on the table?" *ho 'ala tawla*? However, I yet again wish to stress that this isn't a grammar book!

I was - Ana kent
To be - (**M**) Ykun / (**F**) Tikun
The - Al
Same – Nafs alhal
Good - Zain
Here - Hena
Very – Hail / Marra
And - W
Between - Bain
Now – Alheen
Later / After / afterwards - Ba'ad / Ba'den
If - Etha
Yes - Iyeh
To – N/ la
Tomorrow – Bokra / Bacher
You - (M) Ent / (F) Enti
Also / too / as well – Ba'ad
With them – Ma'ahom

If it's between now and later
Etha kan bain alheen w ba'deen
It's better tomorrow
Bokra ahsan
This is good as well
Hatha zain ba'ad
To be the same person
Yekon nafs alshakhs
Yes, you are very good
Eh, ent hail zain
I was here with them
Ana knt hena ma'ahom
You and I
Ent w ana
The same day
Nafs alyom

Me - Le
Ok – Tamam / Kuayis
Even if - Hatta law / Hatha etha
No – lla
Worse – Aswa'
Where - Wain
Everything – Kel shi
Somewhere – Ay mkan
What – Aish? / Shno?
Almost - Tagriban
There - Henak

Afterwards is worse
Ba'aden aswa'
Even if I go now
Hatta law arooh alheen
Where is everything?
Wain kelshai?
Maybe somewhere
Yimken fi makan
What? I am almost there
Aish? Ana taqreban henak
Where are you?
(M) Wheynak? (F) Wheynach?
Where is the airport?
Wain el matar?

*"There" has two meanings, *fe* or *hnak* depending on the context, when we say there is we say *fe* / but when we say "I am there (place)" we say *ana hnak*.
* *makan* literally means *in a place*

*In Arabic, the pronoun "me" has several definitions. In relation to verbs, it's *le*. Le refers to any verb that relates to the action of doing something to someone or for someone.
For example, "tell me," "tell (to) me" / *(M) gool le*.
'ni' just means "me": "love me" / *hebbni*
Other variations (*ya*):
   * "on me" / *'aleya*, "in me" / *fiya*
   * "to me" / *'leya*, "with me" / *ma'aya*
The same rule applies for "him" and "her"—both become suffixes: –*o* and –*a*.
Basically all verbs pertinent to males end with *h*, and all pertinent to female end with ha.
   * "love her" / *ahebha*
   * "love him" / *ahebbah*
   * "love them" / *ahebhom*
   * "love us" / *ahebbna*
Any verb that relates to doing someone to someone, for someone put *l*:
   * "tell her" / *gel-lha*
   * "tell him" / *gel-lh*
   * "tell them" / *gel-lhom*
   * "tell us" / *qel-lna*
Adding you as a suffix in Arabic is *ak* or *lak*, female *ik* or *lik*.
   * "love you" / (M) *ahebbak* / (F) *ahebbech*
   * "tell you" / (M) *agol-lk* / (F) *agol-lch*

House - Bait
In / at - Fe / A'la
Car - Seyyara
Already – Aslan
Good morning - Sabah el kheir
How are you? – Shlonak? (F)Shlonach? Shakhbarek? (F) Shakhbarich?
Where are you from? – (M) Min wain ent? (F) Min wain enti?
Today - Alyom
Hello - Ahlan
What is your name? – (M) Shesmek? (F) Shesmich?
How old are you? - (M) Kam omrak? / (F) Kam omrich?
Son – Wald
Daughter - Bnt
To have – (M)'Endah / (F) 'Endha
Doesn't – Ma / La
Hard – Sa'ab
Still – **(M)** Baqi / (F) Baqia lelheen
Then (or "so") – Ba'ad/ W ba'ad
In order to – 'Ashan

She doesn't have a car, so maybe she is still at the house?
Ma endaha seyyara, yemkin lelheen fel bait?
I am in the car already with your son and daughter
Ana bel/fel seyyara aslan ma'a wldak w bntak
Good morning, how are you today?
Sabah al kheir, (M) Shlonak/(F) Slonach alyoum?
Hello, what is your name?
Hala, (M) Shesmek / (F) Shemich?
How old are you?
Kam omrak/ (F) omrich?
This is very hard, but it's not impossible
Hatha sa'ab heel, bas mub mustaheel
Then where are you from?
Min wain ent?

*In Arabic, possessive pronouns become suffixes to the noun. For example, in the translation for "your," *ak* is the masculine form, and *ich* is the feminine form. *Ich/ach*
  * "your book" / *ktabak* (m.), *ktabik* (f.) *ktabich*
  * "your house" / *baitak* (m.), *baitik* (f.) *baitich*

*In Saudi Arabic *a* is used to indicate cases of "to" or "to be able to." You will notice in the program *ka* will quite often become a prefix to the verb "I want to learn," *ana abe at'alem* or "in order to be able to go", *Ashan agdar arooh*

Ashan means "because of," but it is also used to indicate "so."

Thank you - Mashkur
For – 'Ashan
Anything - Ay Shay / kl shay
That / That is – (F) Hathik / (M) Hathak (F) Theek (M) Thak
Time - Zaman (duration) / Sa'a (if asking about the clock) Wagt (duration)
But - W laken / Bas
No / not - La / Mu
I am not - Ana la / Ma
Away - B'eed
Late – Meta'kher
Similar – Methl / Zay Nafs
Another/ other – Thany / Ghair
Side – Jnb / Yam
Until – Elen / Lain
Yesterday – Elbareh / Ams
Without us – Bdon-na
Since – Min wagt ma
Day - Youm
Before – Gabl

Thanks for everything
Mashkur ala kl Shay
It's almost time
Hatha alwagt tagreban
I am not here, I am away
Ana mub hena, ana b'eed
That is a similar house
Hatha methl albait
I am from the other side
Ana min makan thany
But I was here until late yesterday
Bas ana knt hena len allail ams a'kher
I am not at the other house
Ana mu fe albait althany

*In Arabic *mojood* literally means "to exist" or "is present."
*In Saudi Arabic regarding negations, such as "no", "not", "doesn't", "can't", "don't" it's either *ma* or *la*. *La* is used to indicate cases such as "are you here" ent hena then you reply "no" *la*. is used to indicate cases of "not," "doesn't," "don't," for example: "I am not at the other house" is *ana mu fi albait el athani*. In some instances both cases of *la* may be used, for example; "can you come?" "No I can't" *la ma haqder*.
*In Saudi Arabic, there are three definitions for time:
  * "time" / *mudda* refers to "era", "moment period," "duration of time."
  * "time(s)" / *marra(t)* / wagt *(t)* refers to "occasion" or "frequency."
*"time" / *sa'a* references "hour," "what time is it?" Time, *sa'ah* in reference to; hour, what time is it.
***This isn't a phrase book! The purpose of this book is solely to provide you with the tools to create your own sentences!**

What time is it? – Kam al sa'aa?
I say / I am saying – Agool / Ana agool-lk/ (F) Agool-lch
I want Ana abe / Abe
Without you – (M) Bdoonak / (F) Bedonich
Everywhere /wherever – Kl makan
I go – Barooh
With - Ma'a
My – Le
Cousin (paternal) - (M) Wld 'amy / (F) Bnt 'amy / (P)(F) Banaat 'amy (P)(M) Awlad 'amy/ 'Aiyal 'amy
Cousin (maternal) - (M) Wld khali / (F) Bnt khali / (P)(M) Wlaad khaly / (P)(F) Banaat khaly (P)(M) Awlad khaly/'Aiyal khaly
I need – Ahtaj
Right now – Alheen
Night – Lail
To see – 'Ashan ashoof
Light - Noor
Outside – Barra / 'Ala barra
Without – Bala / Bdoon
Happy – Farhan / Saeed Mistanes
I see / I am seeing – Anadher / Ashoof
I am saying no / I say no - Agool la'

I want to see this today
Abe ashof hatha alyom
I am with you everywhere
Ana (M) ma'ak (F) ma'ach Fe kl makan
I am happy without my cousins here
Ana sa'ed bdoon Awlad 'ammy hna
I need to be there at night
Ahtaj akoon hnak be allail
I see light outside
Ashoof noor barra
What time is it right now?
Kam alsa'aa alheen?

---

*"Mine" /*haggi, maly* is also a possessive pronoun. Haggi/Maly *Haggi* means "my" but also becomes a suffix to a noun. Nouns ending in a vowel end with *–the*. Nouns ending with a consonant end with *–eh*. For example:

"cousin" / *iben el 'amm*, "my cousin" / *iben 'ammy*, "cup" / *cob*, "my cup" / *cobi*
For second and third person masculine noun, *ibin* ("son"), male (S) *ak*, (P) *kom*) and female (S) *ich (P) kum*). "His" – *ilo* / "hers" – *ila*, noun endings will be *o* (for male) and *a* (for female).

"your son" / *ibnak* (m.), *ibnik* (f.), "your (plural) son" / *ibinkom* (m.), *bintkom* (f.), "his son" / *ibnoh*, "her son" / *ibnha*, "our son" / ibnna , "their son" / ibbnhom (m.), ibnnhon(f.)

For second and third person feminine noun: "car" / *seyyara*.
* "your car" / *seyyartek*, "your (plural) car" / *seyyartkom*, "his car" / *seyyartah*, "her car" / *seyyartha*, "our car" / *seyyaratna*, "their car" / *seyyarthom*

Place – Makan
Easy - Sahel
To find - **(M)** Yelga / (F)Telga
To look for / to search – Yedawwer
Near / Close - Garib
To wait – Yestanna / yentdher
To sell - (M) Ybee' - (F) tbee'
To use – Yesta'amel
To know – Y'arf
To decide – Yqarrir
Between - Bain
Both – Thnain
To – 'Ashan (preceding a verb)

This place it's easy to find
Hatha almkan sahel algah
I want to look for this next to the car
Ana abe adawer janb alseyyara
I am saying to wait until tomorrow
Ana agool nentedher len bokra
This table is easy to sell
Hathi altawla sahel tenba'
I want to use this
Abe asta'mel hathi
I need to know where is the house
Ahtaj a'aref wain albait
I want to decide between both places
Abe aqrrer bain almkanen

* *Lazim* means "must" however in this program, both, *lazim* and *ahtaj* will be used interchangeably.
* In Saudi Gulf Arabic, in the event "doesn't" is used regarding negations of verbs, the following requirements must precede and follow *ma.. mat.. ha,* for example: "she doesn't like (The verb "like" is y*e'jeb*) the beer" – *hey ma te'ajbha lbeera.*

Because – 'Ashan
To buy – Ashtry
They - Hum
Them | Their – Hum / Haghum/Malhum/hum
Bottle – Qarora / Gharsha
Book - Kitab
Mine - Haggi
To understand – Yefham
Problem / Problems - (S) Mushkila / Meshakel
I do / I am doing - N'mel / A'amel Asawy
Of - Mn
To look – Yshoof
Myself - Nafsi
Enough – Khalas / Kafi
Food / water - Akil / Moya
Each/ every/ entire/ all – Kl
Hotel - Fondoq

I like this hotel because I want to look at the beach
Ajbni hatha alfondoq ashan weddi ashoof alshate'a
I want to buy a bottle of water
Ana abe ashtry gharshat maay
I do this everyday
Ana asawy chetha kl youm
Both of them have enough food
Ethnenhom endhom akl kafi
That is the book, and that book is mine
Hatha alktab, w hatha alktab haggi
I need to understand the problem
Ana ahtaj afham almushkila
I see the view of the city from the hotel
Ashoof mandhar almadina mn alfondoq
I do my homework today
Asawy wajbati alyoum
My entire life (*all my life*)
Kl hayati / kl omri

I like – Ye'jbni
There is / There are – Fe
Family / Parents - 'Aylah / Walidin / Ahel
Why – Laish
To say – Agool / (M) Ygool / (F) Tgool
Something – Haja / Shai
To go – Nmshy / (M) Yimshy / (F) Timshy
Ready – Jahiz
Soon – Gareeb
To work – Ashteghil / (M) Yeshteghil / (F) Teshteghil
Who – Meen
To know – A'aref
That (conjunction) – Ennah

I like to be at my house with my parents
Aheb akon bilbait ma' ahle
I want to know why I need to say something important
Ana weddi a'aref laish ana ahtaj agool shai mohem
I am there with him
Ana hnak ma'ah
I am busy, but I need to be ready soon
Ana mashghool, bass ahtaj akon jahiz gareb
I like to go to work
Ye'ajbni aroh al amal / alshghl
'Who is there?
Meen hnak?
I want to know if they are here, because I want to go outside
Ana abe a'aref etha hom hena, ashan abe arooh barra / weddi atla'a
There are seven dolls
Fee sab'a al'ab
I need to know that it is a good idea
Ahtaj a'aref ennah fekra zaina

*In the last sentence, we use "that" as a conjunction (*ennah*) and a demonstrative pronoun *(M) hatha* / *(F) theek*).

How much /how many – Kam / Gad esh
To bring – Ajeb
With me – Ma'aya
Instead - Badal
Only – Bass / Lamma
When – Mita
Or – Aw
I can / Can I – Ana agdar / Mumken?/ 'Adey? / Agdar?
Were - Kano
Without me – Bdooni
Fast – Bser'aa
Slow – Batee / Shway / B-shwaysh
Cold – Bard
Inside – Jowwa / Dakhel / Fee
To eat – 'Aakil
Hot – Haar
To Drive – Aswog
To drive - Yasouk

How much money do I need to bring with me?
Kam ajeeb ma'ay floos?
Instead of this cake, I want that cake
Badal hathi al caikah, abe hathi al caikah
Only when you can
Bas etha/lamman tegdar *(etha is more common)*
They were without me yesterday
Hum kanu bdooni ams
Do I need to drive the car fast or slow?
Ahtaj Asoog al seyyara bsr'aa wala bel?
It is cold inside the library
Bard dakhel al-maktabah
Yes, I like to eat this hot for my lunch
Eih, ye'jebny akil haar bil-ghada
I can work today
Agdar asht'eghel alyom

*"Were" is *kanu*, but for "they were," "We were" is *kenna*.

*"I can" and "can I?" is *ana agdar*. "You can" or "can you?" is *ent tegdr?*

To answer – (M)Yejaweb (F) Tejaweb
To fly – Yeteer / Yesafer
Time / Times - Mrra / Mrrat
To travel – Yesafer
To learn - At'allam / (M) Yt'alam / (F) Tet'alam
How – Kif / Sh-loan
To swim - Asbah / (M) Yesbah / (F) Tesbah
To practice – Atmmarran
To play - Al'aab
To leave – Yemshi / Yetla'a / Ykhalli
Many /much /a lot – Ktheer / Wajed
I go to – Amshy / Arooh
First – Al-awl
Time / Times – Mrra/Mrrat

I want to answer many questions
Ana abe ajwaeb as'ila ktheera
I must fly to Dubai today
Ana lazim asafer Dubai alyom
I need to learn how to swim at the pool
Ana ahtaj at'allam kif asbah bil masbah
I want to learn to play better tennis
Abe at'allam al'aab tennis ahsan
I want to leave this here for you when I go to travel the world
Abe atrok hatha hena lk lamman arooh asafer al 'aalamm
Since the first time
Min awl mrra
The children are yours
Al-altfal haggonak

*In Saudi Gulf dialect, "to leave (something)" is (M)Yikhley /(F) Tkhaley/ Akhley. "To leave (a place)" is (M)Yet'la'/ (F) Tet'la'/ At'la'.

*In Gulf dialect, there are three definitions for time:
  - "time" / *mudda* refers to "era", "moment period," "duration of time."
  - "time(s)" / *marra(t)* /refers to "occasion" or "frequency."
  - "time" / *sa'a* references "hour," "what time is it?"

*With the knowledge you've gained so far, now try to create your own sentences!

Nobody / anyone – Mahad / Ay ahad
Against - Dhed
Us – Ehna
To visit - Yzoor
Mom / Mother – Ommi / Yumma
To give – Ye'ty
Which – Ay / Ayt
To meet – Ytqabal / Ytlaga
Someone – Ahad
Just - Bass
To walk - Ytmasha
Around – Hawalin
Towards – Etejah
Than - Min
Nothing – Abad / Mafe shi / Wala shi

Something is better than nothing
Shai ahsan min wala shai
I am against him
Ana dheddah
Is there anyone here?
Fe ahad hena?
We go to visit my family each week
Nrooh nzoor al ahil kl asboo'
I need to give you something
Ahtaj a'atek shai
Do you want to go meet someone?
Taby tgabil ahad?
I was here on Wednesdays as well
Ana kent h ena al arba' ba'ad
Do you do every day
Ent tsawwy hatha kl youm?
You need to walk around, but not towards the house
Ent tehtaj tmshy, bass mub etjiah albait

*In Arabic, when using the pronoun "you" as a direct and indirect object pronoun (the person who is actually affected by the action that is being carried out) in relation to a verb, the pronoun "you" becomes a suffix to that verb. That suffix becomes *ak* (masc.) *ich* (fem.).
  * "to give" / *a'te* "to give you" / *a'teek*
  * "to tell" / *qool*: "to tell you" / qoolak (m.), Agool-lich (f.)
  * "see you" / a*shoofak*: "to see you" (plural) / a*shoofkom* (m.), a*shoofkon* (f.)

For third person male, add *oh* and *hom* for plural, for female add h*a* and h*on* for plural.
  * "tell him" / *gool-lah*
  * "tell her" / *qool-lha*
  * "see them" / *shoofhom* (m.), *shoofhon* (f.)
  * "see us " / *shoofna*

I have – 'Endy
Don't - La
Friend – Saheb / Sadeeg
To borrow – Yetsallaf
To look like / resemble – Yeshbah
Like (preposition) - Shbah
Grandfather – Jad
To want - Yaby
To stay – Yjles / Ybga / Yage'd
To continue – Ystamer
Way – T'areeg
I don't - Ana ma rah
To show - Yewarry
To prepare – Yessawy / yejjahiz
I am not going – Ana mub arooh

Do you want to look like Salim
Tbe tseer teshabah Salim
I want to borrow this book for my grandfather
Abe ate'eer hal ketab hag jaddy
I want to drive and to continue on this way to my house
Abe asooq w astamer 'ala hathak alt'areeg lain-baity
I have a friend there, that's why I want to stay in Riyadh
'andy saheb hnak, ashan ketha weddi agles bel-Riyadh
I am not going to see anyone here
Ana ma rah ashoof ahad hena
I need to show you how to prepare breakfast
Ahtaj awareek kif tessawy alfotoor
Why don't you have the book?
Laish ma e'ndak/ ma'ak al-ktab?
That is incorrect, I don't need the car today
Hatha ghalat, ana ma ahtaj alseyyara al-youm

*In Saudi Arabic the case of "you don't have" is *ma e'ndak* or *ma ma'ak* or *ma 'endy*.

To remember - 'Atthakkar
Your - (M) Tak / (F) tech
Number - Raqm
Hour - Sa'aa
Dark / darkness – Dhalam
About / on the - 'Ala
Grandmother - Jadda / my grandmother – Jaddateya
Five - Khams
Minute / minutes - Dqeeqa / Dqayq
More – Akthar
To think – Yfakker
To do – Yea'mel / Yessawy
To come – Yejy
To hear - Ysma'
Last – Akheer / Akher

You need to remember my number
Tehtaj tet'thakkar raqmy
This is the last hour of darkness
Hathy akher Sa'aa min al lail / aldhalam
I want to come and to hear my grandmother speak Saudi Arabic
Abe ajy w sma' jaddateya tetkalm 'araby Saudi
I need to think more about this, and what to do
Ahtaj afakker fe hatha akthar, w aiysh asawwy
From here to there, it's only five minutes
Min hena le hnak, bass khams dqayq
The school on the mountain
Almadrasa ala al jabal

To leave – Nkhroj / Netla'
Again – Ba'ad / Thanya
Arabic - Arabi
To take - Nakhth
To try – Ajreb / Ahawel
To rent – A'ajer
Without her - Bdonha
We are – Ehna
To turn off - Ytaffy
To ask – Ys'al
To stop - Ywqf
Permission - Ethn

He needs to leave and rent a house at the beach
Hw yhtaj ykhroj w y'ajer bait ala al shate'a
I want to take the test without her
Abe akth al emtehan bdonha
We are here a long time
Ehna hena min wagt toweel
I need to turn off the lights early tonight
Ahtaj at'afey alanwaar badry aleil
We want to stop here
Naby nwgaf hena
We are from Dammam
Ehna min al-dammam
The same building
Nafs alemara / almabna
I want to ask permission to leave
Ana abe ethn ashan atla'
I want to sleep
Ana abe anam

To open - Yeftah
A bit, a little, a little bit - Shway
To pay – Yedfa'
Once again – Mrra thanya
There isn't/ there aren't - Mafi
Sister - Ekht
To hope – Atmna
To live - Y'esh
Nice to meet you – Tsharafna
Name - Esm
Last name – Esm al 'ayla
To return – Yerja'
Door - Baab

I need to open the door for my sister
Ana ahtaj aftah elbaab l-okhty
I need to buy something
Ana ahtaj ashtrey shay
I want to meet your sisters
Ana abe ata'raf a'la okhtak.
Nice to meet you, what is your name and your last name
Tesharrafn, shenu esmak w esm 'eltak?
To hope for a little better
Tmna shwya ahsan
I want to return from the United States and to live in Qatar without problems
Abe arja' min America w a'eesh fe Qatar bdoon meshakel
Why are you sad right now?
'Lesh ent Hazeen / za'laan elhin?
There aren't any people here
Mafe nas hena
There isn't enough time to go to Qatif today
Mafe waqt kafy nmshy al Qatif al-youm

*In Saudi Arabic, regarding the verb "to meet" there are two separate cases to define this verb; *tqabil*. Depending of the context: to meet for business is *agabil* like in the sentence "do you want to go meet someone?" However, for meeting the sister, is getting acquainted with her, here it's tet'araf

*This *isn't* a phrase book! The purpose of this book is *solely* to provide you with the tools to create *your own* sentences!

To happen – Yeseer
To order – Yetlub
To drink -Yeshrab
Excuse me - (M) Law samaht / (F) Law smahati
Child - (M) T'efl (F) T'efla
Woman – Mra / Hurma
To begin / to start - Ybda
To finish - Yentahi
To help – Yesa'ed
To smoke - Yedakhen
To love - Yheb
To talk / to speak – Ytkallam
Gulf Cooperation Council – Majlis al-ta'aiwun al-khaliji

This must happen today
Hatha lazim yeseer l-yom
Excuse me, my child is here as well
Law samaht, ibny hena ba'ad
I love you
Ana ahebak (F) ahebich
I see you
Ana ashoofak (F) ashoofich
I need you at my side
Ahtajak janbi (F) Ahtajich
I need to begin soon to be able to finish at 3 o'clock in the afternoon
Ahtaj abda badri ashan agdar akhalles ala alsa'a 3 aldhuhr
I need help
Ahtaj mosa'ada
I don't want to smoke once again
Ana ma abe adakhen marra thanya
I want to learn how to speak Arabic
Abe at'allam kaif atkallam arabi

*"To be able to" is *agdar-word- ex. To be able to learn - agdar at'allam.*

To read - Yeqra
To write - Yektob
To teach – Y'allem
To close – Yegaffel
To choose - Yekhtar
To prefer - Yefaddill
To put - Yehott
Less - Agal
Sun - Shamss
Month - Shahr
I talk - Atkalm
Exact – Tamam / Bel-zhabt'

I need this book to learn how to read and write in Arabic because I want to teach in Egypt
Ahtaj hatha al-ktaab ashan at'allam kaif agra w aktob bel 'araby ashan abe addarres fe masser.
I want to close the door of the house
Abe assakker baab albeit
I prefer to put the gift here
afaddill ahott al hadeya hena
I want to pay less than you for the dinner
Abe adfaa' agal minnak lel-'asha
I speak with the boy and the girl in French
Ana atkalm ma' alwlad w albentt bill faransi
There is sun outside today
Fi shamss barra l-yom
Is it possible to know the exact date?
Momken te'aref alwaqt Bel-zhabt'?

*"For the" is *le al*

*"In" is *be al / fe al*

*With the knowledge you've gained so far, now try to create your own sentences!

To exchange (money) – Yehawwel
To call – Yenade
Brother – Akh
Dad – 'Ab
To sit – Yejles / Yag'ed
Together – Sawa / Ma' ba'adh
To change – Yeghayyer
Of course - Tab'an / Akeed
Welcome – Hala
During - Athna
Years - (**S**)'Aam / Sana / (**P**) 'A'waam / Sineen
Sky - Sama
Up – Foq
Down - Taht
Sorry - Aseff
To follow - Yelhag
To the – Le / Lain
Big – Kabeer
New – Jadeed
Never / ever - 'Omry ma / Abad / Ma gad

I don't want to exchange this money at the bank
Ana ma abe ahhawwel al flos fel-bank
I want to call my brother and my dad today
Ana abe 'akallim akhoy w aboy al-youm
Of course I can come to the theater, and I want to sit together with you and with your sister
Akeed agdar aje a'l massrah, w ana abe njles sawa ma'ak w ma' okhtak
I need to go down to see your new house
Abe arooh ashoof baytik al jdeed
I can see the sky from the window
Agdar ashof alsama min alnafetha / aldreesha
I am sorry, but he wants to follow her to the store
Ana aseff, bas ho yabi yelhag'ha len almahal
I don't ever want to see you again
Ma abe ashofak Thanyea abad

*In Saudi Gulf dialect, brother is *akh*, and dad is *ab*. However, "my dad" is *abooy* and "my brother" is a*khoy*. "My sister" is e*khtey*, and "my mother" is *ommi*

*For the possessive pronouns, her *(ha)* and him *(ah)*, both become suffixes to the verb or noun. Concerning nouns: her house / *baitha*, his house / *baitah* Concerning verbs please see page #19.

To allow - Yesmah
To believe – Yesaddeg
Morning – Sbaah
Except - Ma 'ada / Ella
To promise - Yw'ed
Good night – Tesbah ala khair
To recognize - Ye'araf
People - Naas
To move - Yharrek
Far - B'eed
Different – ghair
Man - rajjal
To enter - Yedkhal
To receive – Yestagbil / Yakhoth
Throughout – Min bain
Good evening – Masaa' alkheir
Left / right - Ysar / Ymeen

I need to allow him to go with us, he is a different man now
Ahtaj akhallih yeje m'aana, ho rajjal thany alhen
I believe everything except this
Ana asaddig kl shai ela hatha
I promise to say good night to my parents each night
Wa'ad eni agol tesbah ala khair le ahli kl laila
The people from Jordan are very pleasant
Alnas min alordon hlailen
I need to find another hotel very quickly
Ahtaj alga/ahhassel fondog thany bsr'aa
They need to receive a book for work
Hom yehtajoon yakhtho alkitab lel'amal
I see the sun in the morning
Ana ashoof alshams fil-sabah
The house is on the right side of the street
Albeit ala aljanb alyamen min alshare'

To wish - Atmanna
Bad – Saye'e
To get - Akhoth
To forget - Ansa
Everybody / Everyone - Kl shakhs
Although – Ma'a enna
To feel - Ahiss
Great – Zain
Next (as in close, near) - Janb
Next (as in next year) - Jai
To like – A'ajab
In front – Qeddam
Person - Shakhs
Behind – Khalf / Wara
Well – Zain / Kuwaies
Restaurant – Mata'am
Bathroom – Hammam
Goodbye – Ma' alsalama

I don't want to wish you anything bad
Ana ma atmana lak ay shay mo zaina
I must forget everybody from my past to feel well
Ana bansa kl shaks min al madhy a'shan ahess ahsan
I am next to the person behind you
Ana janb al shakhs ally warak
There is a great person in front of me
Fi shakhs a'dheem gedammy
I say goodbye to my friends
Ana aqoul ma' alsalama l asdega'e
Where is the bathroom in the restaurant?
Wain alhammam bill mata'am?
She has to get a car before the next year
He lazim tjeb seyyara qabl alsana al jaia
I like the house, but it is very small
Ajbni albeit, bass marra sagher

janb literally means "side." In Arabic, it refers to "next." *janb* is "besides me" and *janbak* is "besides you."

To remove / to take out - Yeshel
Please - Takfa
Beautiful - (**M**)Mzyon, (**F**)Jameela
To lift – Yerfa'
Include / Including - Yeshmal
Belong – Yantami le
To hold - Yemsak
To check – Yeraje' / Yeta'akad
Small – Sagheer
Real - Haqeeqy
Week – Esboo'
Size – Hajm / Magas
Even though – Hatta law
Doesn't – Ma
So (as in "then") – Ya'ny / W baa'den
So (as in "so big") – Marra / Heel
Price – Thaman / Se'er

She wants to remove this door please
He taby tsheel ha-albab law samaht
This doesn't belong here, I need to check again
Hatha mkanh mu hna, ahtaj at'akad mrra thanya
This week the weather was very beautiful
Hatha alesboo' aljaw heel helo
I need to know which is the real diamond
Ahtaj a'aref ay almasa el-hqeeqya
We need to check the size of the house
Nehtaj neshoof hajm albait
I want to lift this, so you need to hold it high
Abe ashel hatha, ya'ny lazim temsakah fog
I can pay this even though that the price is expensive
Agdar adfa' hatha hatta law alse'er ghali
Including everything is this price correct?
Shamel kl shi hatha alse'er sah?

Countries of the Middle East
Duoal al-sharq al- awsatt

Lebanon - Lobnan
Syria - Suriyya
Jordan - L-ordon
Saudi Arabia - al-so'odya
Israel /Palestine /West Bank - Isra'eel / Falasteen / al-daffa algharbiyya
Bahrain - l-Bahrein
Yemen - l-Yaman
Oman - 'Oman
United Arab Emirates - l-Emarat al'arabya el-motaheda
Kuwait - l-Kwait
Iraq - l-Iraq
Qatar - Qatar
Morocco - al-maghreb
Algeria - l-Jazayer
Libya - Leebya
Egypt - Masser
Tunisia – Tunes

Months
January - ynayr
February - febrayr
March – mares
April - ebreel
May - may
June – Yuniu
July – Yuliu
August - aughustus
September – September
October - oktobar
November - november
December - december

Colors
Black - aswad
White - **abyad**h
Gray - Rmaddi
Red - **a**hamr
Blue - azraq
Yellow - asfar
Green - akhdhar
Orange – brtgali
Purple - banfsaji
Brown –bonni

Numbers
One - Wahed
Two - thnen
Three – Thlath
Four - arb'aa
Five – Khams
Six - Sitt
Seven - Sab'a
Eight - Thman
Nine – Tis'a
Ten - 'Ashr
Twenty - 'Eshreen
Thirty - Thlathen
Thirty - Talateen
Forty - Arb'in
Fifty - Khamseen
Sixty - Sitteen
Seventy - Sab'een
Eighty - Tamaneen
Ninety - Tis'een
Hundred - Miyya
Thousand – Alf
Million - Million

Days of the Week
Sunday - al- ahad
Monday - al-athnen
Tuesday - al-tholatha'
Wednesday - al-arbe'aa'
Thursday - al-khamees
Friday - jom'aa
Saturday - Sabt

Seasons
Spring – Rabee'
Summer - Seif
Autumn - Khareef
Winter - Shetta

Cardinal Directions
North - Shamaal
South - Janoob
East – Sharq
West - Gharb

Conversational Arabic Quick and easy

QATARI DIALECT

YATIR NITZANY

THE QATARI DIALECT

The population of Qatar is 2.6 million, and there has been a great influx of English along with globalization and the expatriates who live there.

Arabic is the official language of Qatar, and Qatari Arabic is the country's local dialect. Gulf Arabic or Khaliji is also spoken in Qatar, as well as Modern Standard Arabic, which is the official language of the government and of printed materials. Gulf Arabic is also spoken in Bahrain, Kuwait, Saudi Arabia, and the United Arab Emirates.

Gulf Arabic varieties are not completely mutually intelligible with other Arabic varieties spoken outside the Gulf. The specific dialects differ in vocabulary, grammar, and accent. There are considerable differences, especially in accent, between, for example, Kuwaiti Arabic and the dialects of Qatar and the UAE, which may hinder mutual understanding.

There is also a Qatari dialect called Nabati, which is a derivative of classical Arabic and has been used for poetry and culture. It has been shaped by the local context.

Teaching in Qatar, as with other Gulf states, had begun to take place more and more in English with the consequence that Arabic was seen to be weakening. A change was formulated, therefore, in an effort to strengthen Arabic and particularly the Qatari dialect. Streets and areas were renamed and some regained their original names while others' spelling was reformulated so it could be pronounced in the Qatari dialect. For example, the Old Rayyan area used to be called Al-Rayyan Al-Qadim but has now been changed to Al-Rayyan Al-Aateeq, its original name.

Also, Qatari license plates are now written in Arabic numbers instead of the earlier Indian-origin numbers, while another step has been to reintroduce communication between ministries in Arabic.

The local Qatari dialect is being revived and brought back through usage in different areas and attempts to revive the dynamics of the language.

Spoken in: Qatar

MEMORIZATION MADE EASY

There is no doubt the three hundred and fifty words in my program are the required essentials in order to engage in quick and easy basic conversation in any foreign language. However, some people may experience difficulty in the memorization. For this reason, I created Memorization Made Easy. This memorization technique will make this program so simple and fun that it's unbelievable! I have spread the words over the following twenty pages. Each page contains a vocabulary table of ten to fifteen words. Below every vocabulary box, sentences are composed from the words on the page that you have just studied. This aids greatly in memorization. Once you succeed in memorizing the first page, then proceed to the second page. Upon completion of the second page, go back to the first and review. Then proceed to the third page. After memorizing the third, go back to the first and second and repeat. And so on. As you continue, begin to combine words and create your own sentences in your head. Every time you proceed to the following page, you will notice words from the previous pages will be present in those simple sentences as well, because repetition is one of the most crucial aspects in learning any foreign language. Upon completion of your twenty pages, congratulations, you have absorbed the required words and gained a basic, quick-and-easy proficiency and you should now be able to create your own sentences and say anything you wish in the Qatari Arabic dialect. This is a crash course in conversational Arabic, and it works!

ARABIC PRONUNCIATIONS

PLEASE MASTER THE FOLLOWING PAGE IN ARABIC PRONUNCIATIONS PRIOR TO STARTING THE PROGRAM

Kha. For Middle Eastern languages including Arabic, Hebrew, Farsi, Pashto, Urdu, Hindi, etc., and also German, to properly pronounce the kh or ch is essential, for example, *Khaled* (a Muslim name) or *Chanukah* (a Jewish holiday) or *Nacht* ("night" in German). The best way to describe kh or ch is to say "ka" or "ha" while at the same time putting your tongue at the back of your throat and blowing air. It's pronounced similarly to the sound that you make when clearing your throat. Please remember this whenever you come across any word containing a kh in this program.

Ghayin. The Arabic gh is equivalent to the "g" in English, but its pronunciation more closely resembles the French "r," rather than "g." Pronounce it at the back of your throat. The sound is equivalent to what you would make when gargling water. Gha is pronounced more as "rha," rather than as "ga." *Ghada* is pronounced as "rhada." In this program, the symbol for *ghayin* is gh, so keep your eyes peeled.

Aayin is pronounced as a'a, pronounced deep at the back of your throat. Rather similar to the sound one would make when gagging. In the program, the symbol for *aayin* is *a'a, u'u, o'o,* or *i'i*.

Ha is pronounced as "ha." Pronunciation takes place deep at the back of your throat, and for correct pronunciation, one must constrict the back of the throat and exhale air while simultaneously saying "ha." In the program, this strong h ("ha") is emphasized whenever *ha, ah, hi, he,* or *hu* is encountered.

NOTE TO THE READER

The purpose of this book is merely to enable you to communicate in the Qatari Arabic dialect. In the program itself (pages 17-38) you may notice that the composition of some of those sentences might sound rather clumsy. This is intentional. These sentences were formulated in a specific way to serve two purposes: to facilitate the easy memorization of the vocabulary and to teach you how to combine the words in order to form your own sentences for quick and easy communication, rather than making complete literal sense in the English language. So keep in mind that this is not a phrase book!

As the title suggests, the sole purpose of this program is for conversational use only. It is based on the mirror translation technique. These sentences, as well as the translations are not incorrect, just a little clumsy. Latin languages, Semitic languages, and Anglo-Germanic languages, as well as a few others, are compatible with the mirror translation technique.

Many users say that this method surpasses any other known language learning technique that is currently out there on the market. Just stick with the program and you will achieve wonders!

81

Note to the Reader

Again, I wish to stress this program is by no means, shape, or form a phrase book! The sole purpose of this book is to give you a fundamental platform to enable you to connect certain words to become conversational. Please also read the "Introduction" and the "About Me" section prior to commencing the program.

In order to succeed with my method, please start on the very first page of the program and fully master one page at a time prior to proceeding to the next. Otherwise, you will overwhelm yourself and fail. Please do not skip pages, nor start from the middle of the book.

It is a myth that certain people are born with the talent to learn a language, and this book disproves that myth. With this method, anyone can learn a foreign language as long as he or she follows these explicit directions:

* Memorize the vocabulary on each page

* Follow that memorization by using a notecard to cover the words you have just memorized and test yourself.

* Then read the sentences following that are created from the vocabulary bank that you just mastered.

* Once fully memorized, give yourself the green light to proceed to the next page.

Again, if you proceed to the following page without mastering the previous, you are guaranteed to gain nothing from this book. If you follow the prescribed steps, you will realize just how effective and simplistic this method is.

The Program

Let's Begin! "Vocabulary" (Memorize the Vocabulary)

I | I am - Ana
With you – (Male)Ma'ak / (Female)Ma'ach
With him / with her - M Ma'ah/Wayah /F ma'aha/Wayaha
For you – (M) Lik/ (F) Lech
Without him - Bedonah
Without them - Bedonhom
Always - Dayem/ Kel Marra
Was - Kan
This, This is – Hai
Is, it's, it is – Hai, Haza(M)/Haze(F)
Sometimes - Ahyanaan, maraat
Maybe – Yimkin
You, you are, are you - (m) Enta / (f) enti
You (plural) – Antum / entu (both can be used interchangeably)
Better - Ahsan
He, he is - Howa
She, she is – Heya
From - Men
With us - Way'ana / Ma'ana

Sentences composed from the vocabulary

I am with you
Ana Ma'ak (M) / Ana Ma'ach (F)
This is for you
Hai Lak (M) / Hai Lach (F)
I am from Doha
Ana men el doha
Are you from Qatar?
Enta /ente men Qatar?
Sometimes you are with us at the mall
Marrat Takoon Ma'ana Fil Mall
I am always with her
Ana dayem wayaha/Ma'aha
Are you without them today?
Enta / ente bedounhom el youm
Sometimes I am with him
Marrat ana akon ma'ah / wayah

I was - Ana Kent
To be - (**M**) Yukun / (**F**) tkun
The - ll, al
Same / like *(as in similar)* – Nafs, mithal
Good - Zayn
Here - Ehne
Very - Wa'id
And - Wa
Between - Bain
Now - Elhin
Later / After / afterwards – Ba'din
If - Idha
Yes - Na'am, ee
To - Lal, la
Tomorrow - Bokra
Person – Shakhs
Also / too / as well - Ba'ad

If it was between now and later
Idha kan bain elheen wa badain
This is good as well
Hai Ba'ad zain
To be the same person
Tkoon nafs el shakhis
Yes, you are very good
Ee ent wa'id zain
I was here with them
Ana kent hene Ma'ahum
You and I
Enta wa ana
The same day
Nafs elyoum

* In the Arabic language adjectives precede the noun. For example, "the same day" is *nafs el youm*, "small house" is *beit zgeer*, "tall person" is *wa'id taweel*, and "short person" is *wa'id gaseer*.

* In this program the article "the" / *il, al* will sometimes become a prefix at the beginning of the noun. For nouns beginning with *d, n, r, s, sh, t, th,* and *z* the *L,* is omitted and replaced with the initial consonant of the following noun. "the people" / *il–nas is i-nas,* and "the nile" / *il – nil* is *inil.* It is dropped when spoken, however when written it's usually *il-nas* or *il-nil.*

* In this program, to signify "this" and "that" we will use *thak* (m), *hadi* (f) / "this" and *thakk* (m), *hathik* (f) / "that."

Me - Ana, li (read footnote)
Ok – Ok
Even if - Hatta law
No - Laa
Worse - Kha'is
Where – Wein
Everything – Kel shay
Somewhere – Fi makan
What – Shno/wesh
Almost - Tagriban
There - Hnak
I go - Ana barooh
Doesn't / isn't / not - Ma /mosh / mo *(read footnote)*

Afterwards is worse
Ba'dain baseer kha'is
Even if I go now
Hatta law barooh al heen
Where is everything?
Wain kel shay
What? I am almost there
Wesh? ana tagreeban wosalt
Where are you?
Ant wain? (M) / ent wain? (F)
Where is the hospital?
Wain el mostashfa
Where is the embassy?
Wain el safara

*In Qatari Arabic, there are a few ways of expressing negations; *laa*, *mosh*, *ma*. Depending on where they fall in the sentence. For verbs we use *ma* or *mosh*, "I don't want" /*ana ma abi*. Regarding non-verbs, we use *mo*, "I am not here" / *ana mo hne*. But to simply say "no" we use *laa*, for example if asked something like, "are you going?" you would answer, *laa*, to indicate "no."

*In Qatari Arabic the pronoun "me" has several definitions, in relation to verbs it's *ni, li*.
Li refers to any verb that relates to action of doing something to someone, for someone. For example
"Tell me", "tell (to) me" / *gul'li*
Li just means "me":
"love me" / *hibbini*, "on me" / *alay*, "in me" / *fiyyi*, "to me" / *ili*
"With me" / *ma'ai*, "in front of me" / *qbali*, "from me" / *mini*
The same rule applies for "him" and "her," both become suffixes; *hu* and *ha*;
"Love her" / *ahebaha*, "love him" / *ahibah*, "love them" / *ahibahum*, "love us" / *ahibna* Any verb that relates to doing something to someone, for someone put L:
"Tell me"/ *gul li* "tell him"/ *Gullah* "tell her"/ *gullaha* "tell them" *gullahum* "tell us"/*gullana*
Adding "you" as a suffix in Qatari Arabic is *ak* or *lak*. (female) *ech*
"Love you" / (M) *ahibbak*, (F) *ahibbek*/ "tell you" / (M) *agolak* (F) *agolech*

House – Bait / daar
In, at, at the, in the – Fi/bil / Fil
How are you? – **M.** Kefk/**F.** Kefch / Aish Lonak (M) / Aish Lonach (F) (widely used)
Car - Sayyarah
Already – Aslan
Good morning - Sabah el khair
Where are you from? - Mn wain enta?/Ent min wain?
What is your name? – Sheno esmak?/Shesmak
Today - Elyom
Hello – Ahlen
How old are you? – Kam omrak (M) / kam omrach (F)
Son – Weld
Daughter – Bent
To have - (m) Induh –(f) indaha
Hard - Sa'ab
Still – Lain al heen

She doesn't have a car, maybe she is still at the house?
Heya/Hey ma endaha sayara, heya/hey yemken lain al heen fi el bait?
I am in the car already with your son and daughter
Ana fe el sayarah aslan ma'aa weldk w bentk
Good morning, how are you today?
Sabah el khier, kefk/kefch el youm?
Hello, what is your name?
Ahlen shno/shesmak esmak?
How old are you?
Kam omrak?
This is very hard, but it's not impossible
Hada/Hai wa'id sa'ab, laken mo mostaheel
Where are you from?
Mn wain enta?

*In Qatari Arabic, possessive pronouns become suffixes to the noun. For example, in the translation for "your," *ak* is the masculine form and *ik* feminine form.
  * "your book" / *ktabak* (m.), *ktabich* (f.)
  * "your house" / *baitak* (m.), *baitich* (f.)
*In the Arabic language, as well as in other Semitic languages, the article "a" doesn't exist. "She doesn't have a car" / *ehya ma indha sayyarah*.
*The definition of *khalas* can also be "done" or "finished."

**Ashan* means "because of," but it is also used to indicate "so."

Thank you – Shokran
For – Hag
Anything – Ay shai
That, that is – (m) Thakk, (f) hathik
Time - Wagat
But – Bas/Lakin
No – Laa
I am not – Ana ma / mo
Away – Ba'eed
Late – Motaakher
Similar, like – Methl /nafs
Another / other – Thani
Side – Janab /soob
Until – Layn
Yesterday – Ams
Without us – Bedoona
Since – Min
Day – Youm
Before – Gabel

Thanks for anything
Shokran ala ay shay
I am not here, I am away
Ana mosh/mo mojood/hene, ana ba'eed
That is a similar house
Thak nafs el bait
I am from the other side
Ana men el janb el thani
But I was here until late yesterday
Lakin ana kent mojood/hene layn ams
I am not at the other house
Ana mob fil bait thani

*In Qatari Arabic there are 3 definitions for time:
 Time, *wagt* refers to; era, moment period, duration of time.
 Time(s), *marra(t)* refers to; occasion or frequency.
 Time, *sa'ah* in reference to; hour, what time is it.
*In Arabic *mojood* literally means "to exist" or "is present."

I say / I am saying – Ana bgool/bgool
What time is it? - Sa'aa kam? / is'aa kam?
I want – Ana Abi
Without you – Bedonek
Everywhere / wherever – Fe kel makan
I am going – Ana rayeh
With – Ma'a
My – Hagi, li
Cousin – (m) Ibn a'ammy, ibn khali, (f) bent a'ammy, bent khalti
I need – Ana ahtaj, lazim
Right now – Elhin
Night – Fil layl
To see – Yshof
Light – Daw / layt
Outside – Bel kharej / barra
Without - Bedon
I see / I am seeing – Ana bshoof
Happy – Farhan

I am saying no/I say no
Ana bgool la'aa
I want to see this today
Ana abi ashoof hai el-youm
I am with you everywhere
Ana ma'ak f kel makan
I am happy without my cousin here
Ana Farhan bedon ibn a'ammy heni
I need to be there at night
Ana lazim akoon hinak fil layl
I see light outside
Ana ashoof layt barra
What time is it right now?
Sa'aa kam al-heen

* "My, mine" / *li* is also a possessive pronoun. *Li* means "my" but also becomes a suffix to a noun. Nouns ending in a vowel end with *–ti*. Nouns ending with a consonant end with *–y*.
For example; cousin / *owlad il'am*, my cousin / *ibn ammy* or "cup" / *kaseh*, "my cup" / *kasti*.
- For second and third person masculine noun; ibn, "son." (M); *ak, akum/* (F); *ik, ikum* "your son" / (M)*ibnak* (F)*ibnik*, "your (plural) son" / (M)*ibinhum* (F)*binthum*, "his son" / *ibnu*, her son / *ibnha*, "our son" / *ibinnaa* (M) and (F), "their son" / *ibinhum*.
- For second and third person we use feminine noun; car, *sayyarahh*; "your car" / *sayyartak*/ "your (plural) car" / *sayyaritkum*, "his car" / *sayyartu*, "her car" / *sayyarit-ha*, "our car" / *sayyaritna* (M) and (F), "their car" / *sayyarithum*.
- In Qatari, unlike Classical Arabic, plural female is not different from plural male.
* *Lazim* means "must" however in this program, both, *lazim* and *ahtaj* will be used interchangeably.
*This isn't a phrase book! The purpose of this book is solely to provide you with the tools to create your own sentences!

Place - Makan
Easy – Sahl
To find – Ylagi/tlagi
To look for/to search - Ydawwir
Near / Close - Gareeb
To wait - Yentether
To sell – Ybi'i
To use - Yista'mil
To know - Yi'raf
To decide - Ygarrir
Between - Bain
Next to – Janb
To – Li

This place it's easy to find
Hai il-makan sahel tlagy
I want to look for this next to the car
Ana abi adawer hai janeb el sayarrah
I am saying to wait until tomorrow
Ana agol inter lain bokra
This table is easy to sell
Hai el-tawila sahl nabiha
I want to use this
Ana abi asta'mil hai
I need to know where is the house
Ana abi a'arif wein el-bait
I want to decide between the places
Ana abi atagarrar bain makanain

Because – La' anna / ashan
To buy - Yeshtari
Life – Hayah/'omr
Them, they - Hom, Hom
Bottle – Gharsha
Mine – Haggi / Mali
To understand - Yefham
Problem / Problems - Mushkelh/ mashakel
I do / I am doing - Ana usawwi
Of - Min
To look - Yashoof
Myself - Nafsi
Enough - Bekaffi
Food / water - Akl / Moyah / Mai
Each/ every/ all /entire – Kul / kel
Hotel - Fundug, otel
Both – Itnain
Like this – Kidah /chithi (Chithi is very rarely used in Qatar)

I like this hotel because I want to look at the beach
Ana Baheb Hai el Fundug ashan abi ashoof ala-shate
I want to buy a bottle of water
Ana abi ashtari gharshat moya
I do it like this every day
Ana asawi chithi/kidah kul/kel yom
Both of them have enough food
Itnain athom endahom akal bekafi
That is the book, and that book is mine
Hathak el kitab, wa hadhak el kitab haggy
I need to understand the problem
Ana abi afham al mushkilah
I see the view of the city from the hotel
Ana bashoof manzar il madineh min il Fundug
I do my homework today
Ana asawwi wajibi el youm
My entire life/ all my life
Hayati kullaha

*Toul literally means "the length of."
*"Bottle of water" / *gharshat moya*, the use of "of" isn't always required in Arabic.
*Chithi means "like this" or "this way."

I like - Ana bahib/ Ana Yi'gibni
There is / There are – Fi / yojad
Family / Parents - Ahl
Why - Laish
To say - Yegul
Something – Shai
To go – Yroh
Ready - Jahiz
Soon –Ba'ad shuwai
To work - A'mil/Asawwi
Who – Meen / menou
Busy – Mashgul / mo fathy
That (conjunction) - Ena
I Must - Ana lazim
Important – Muhim

I like to be at my house with my parents
Ana bahib/ahib akun fil bayt ma'a ahli
I want to know why I need to say something important
Ana abi a'rif laish lazim agoul shai muhim
I am there with her
Ana hnak wayaha / ma'aha
I am busy, but I need to be ready soon
Ana mashghul, bas lazim akoon jahiz ba'ad shuwai
I like to go to work
Ana bahib aruh ash-shughul/ al-dawam
Who is there?
Min hnak?
I want to know if they are here, because I want to go outside
Ana abi a'aref etha, hom mojoudeen la'anna abi atla'a bara
There are seven dolls
Fi sab'a arousaat
I need to know that that is a good idea
Ana lazim a'rif ena hai fikrah zaina

*In the last sentence, we use "that" as a conjunction (*ena*) and as a demonstrative pronoun (*hai*).
Bisur'ah literally means "quickly."
*In Qatari Arabic, "to go" is *yruh*, however "to go out" is *atla'* bara.

How much /How many – Kam
To bring – Yib
With me - Ma'ai
Instead – Badal men
Only - Bas
When – Lamma / Mata
I can / Can I? - Ana bagdar / agdar
Or - Walla/aw
Were – Kan
Without me – Bedoni
Fast - Saree'
Slow - Bateei'
Cold – Barid
Cold weather - Jaw barid
Inside - Dakhel
To eat - Yakel
Hot – Har
To drive - Yasouk

How much money do I need to bring with me?
Kam floos lazim ayib ma'ayi?
Instead of this cake, I want that cake
Badal hai elkekeh, abi thak elkek
Only when you can
Bas lamma tigdar
They were without me yesterday
Hom kanou Bedoni ams
Do I need to drive the car fast or slow?
Ana lazim asouk el sayyarah saree'e walla bate'e?
It is cold inside the library
Bard dakhel el maktabah
Yes, I like to eat this hot for my lunch
Ee ana ahib akel hai har le ghadaya
I can work today
Ana agdar ashtaghil elyom

*"Were" / kam, but for "they were," add the suffix to the pronoun, *kanou*. "We were" is *kunna*.
*In Qatari Arabic, *il jaw* means "the climate, weather, temperature, etc."
*In Qatari Arabic, the literal translation of *kam el floos* is "how much money."
*In Qatari Arabic, "money" can be either *floos*.

To answer - Yjeeb
To fly - Ytir
Time / Times – Wagt / awgaat
To travel - Ysafir
To learn - Yit'allam
How – Kaif / Aish lon
To swim -Yisbah
To practice - Yidarrab
To play -Yil'ab
I go to - Ana rayih ala
First - Awwal
World - Alam
Around - Haawl
To leave (something) - Yitrok
Many /much /a lot – Kilosh / Kateer

I want to answer many questions
Ana abi ajawob kel al as'ilah
I must travel to Saudi Arabia today
Ana Lazim asafir le Saudya elyom
I need to learn to swim at the pool
Ana ahtaj at'allam asbah fil birka
I want to learn to play better tennis
Ana abi at'allam al'ab tennis ahsan
I want to leave this here for you when I go to travel the world
Ana abi atrok, hai indak lamma asafir haawl il-alam
Since the first time
Min awwal marrah
The children are yours
Al awlad lek

*In Qatari Arabic, "to leave (something)" is *ytrok*. "To leave (a place)" is *yaroh*.

*In Qatari Arabic there are 3 definitions for time:
-Time, *wagt* refers to; era, moment period, duration of time.
-Time(s), *marra(t)* refers to; occasion or frequency.
-Time, *sa'ah* in reference to; hour, what time is it?

Hathul literally means "those" but again, when we want to say "the children are yours" in Qatari, we say *hathul 'eyalak*, meaning "the children in question" or "the children referred to."

***With the knowledge you've gained so far, now try to create your own sentences!**

Nobody / anyone - Wala ahad / ay ahad
Against - Did
Us - Hnna
To visit - Yizoor
Mom / Mother - Mama / yumma
To give – Yati
Which - Ay
To meet – Yetigabel
Someone – Ahad
Just - Bas
To walk - Yemshi
Week - Usbu'u
Towards - Bittijah
Than - Min
Nothing - Wala shai

Something is better than nothing
Shay ahsan min wala shai
I am against her
Ana didha
We go to visit my family each week
Hnna binzur ahale kul usbu'u
I need to give you something
Ana lazim ateek shai
Do you want to go meet someone?
Tabi taroh tagabel ahad
I was here on Wednesdays as well
Hatta Ana kunt hne al-arbi'a
Do you do this every day?
Inta tusawwi hai kel yom
You need to walk, but not towards the house
Enta lazim tamshi, bas mo tejah el bayt

---

*In Qatari Arabic when using the pronoun "you" as a direct and indirect object pronoun (the person who is actually affected by the action being carried out) in relation to a verb, the pronoun, "you", becomes a suffix to that verb. That suffix becomes (Masc)*ak* (Fem)*ik*. "To give", *yati* / "to give you", *yatik* / "to tell", *yigul* / "to tell you", (M)*yigullak* (F)*yigullech*. "See you", *Ashufak* / "to see you(plural)", (M)*ashufkum*, (F)*ashufkum*. In Qatari they address males and females the same.
For third person male add "*u*" (plural)*hum* and for female add "*ha*" (plural)*hum*. "Tell him" *agullu* / "tell her", *agullaha* / "see them", (M)*ashufhum* (F)*ashufhum* / "see us", *shufna*.
*The definition of *i'mal chithi* is "do this" or "do it like this."

I have - Ana endi
Friend - Rifig
To borrow - Yesta'ir
To look like / resemble - Yishbah
Grandfather - Yid
To want –Abi
To stay – Ythal / atim
To continue - Ykammil
Way (road, path) - Tarig
To show –Yuwari
To prepare - Yjahhiz
I am not going - Ana mob rayeh
Way (method) - Tariga
I don't - Ana ma

Do you want to look like Salim
Tabi taseer mithal salim
I want to borrow this book for my grandfather
Ana abi asta'ir hai kitab le yidi
I want to drive and to continue on this way to my house
Ana abi asouk wa kammil ala hai attareek lil bayti
This isn't the way to do this
Hai mob attareeka ashan tusawwi hai
I have a friend there, that's why I want to stay in Al Wakra
Ana indi sadig / rafij hnak, ashan abi athal / atim (used more than adal) fi-Al Wakra
I am not going to see anyone here
Ana ma rah ashoof ay had hnee
I need to show you how to prepare breakfast
Ana lazim awarik aishlon tusawwi el futoor
Why don't you have the book?
Laish ma indak liktab?
That is incorrect, I don't need the car today
Hai mob sahih, ana ma ahtaj il-sayyarah elyom

*_Sahih_ means "correct"; however, _mo sahih_ means "incorrect."
*_Endak_ means "to have." "I have" is _ana indi_. However, "I don't have" is _Ana ma indi_.
*_Lahad_ means "up to" or "to" as the final destination. It can also mean "until."
*In Qatari Arabic, "to want" is _yabi_
 "I want" / _abi_ "he wants" / _yabi_ "she wants" / _tabi_
*_Tseer_ means "become."
*_Rah_ means "went," indicating future tense, _ana baroh_/ "I will."

To remember – Yit-thakar
Your - Lak
Number - Ragm
Hour - Sa'ah
Dark / darkness – Thalaam
About / on the - 'An/ alal
Grandmother – Yaddah / jaddah
Five - Khamsa
Minute / minutes - Digigah/dagayig
More - Akthar
To think – Itfakker
To do - Asawwi
To come - Yiji
To hear - Yisma'a
Last - Akhir
To talk / to speak – Atakalam

You need to remember my number
Int tahtaj ti-thakkar ragmi
This is the last hour of darkness
Hai akhir sa'a ala athalam
I want to come to hear my grandmother speak Arabic
Abi aji ashan asma jaddati tatakalam arabi
I need to think more about this, and what to do
Ahtaj ufakkir akthar an hai, wa shasawwi
From here to there, it's only five minutes
Min hne layn hnak he bas khamis dagayig
The school on the mountain
Al Madrasah ala jabal

**Mawdoo*' literally means "topic," "subject."
*In Spoken Arabic, "on" is '*ala*, and "the" is *al*. If you were to write it in Arabic, *ala* ("on") and *al* ("the") are separate, but because Qatari make them sound like one word when they utter them, the *ala* and *al* are joined, and it becomes '*alal*.

To leave (to go) – Yemshi / Yarooh
Again - Marah thanyah
Arabic - Arabi
To take - Yakhud
To try - Yjarrib
To rent - Yesta'jir / Ya'jar
Without her – Bedonha
We are - Ehnna
To turn off – Yitfi.
To ask - Yes'al
To stop - Ywagif
Permission - Ithn
Early –Badree
While – Fatra

He needs to leave and rent a house at the beach
Huwwi yahtaj yatrek wa yesta'ager bayt ala al shate'
I want to take the test without her
Ana abi akhod el emtehan bedonha
We are here a long while
Ehna heni min fatrah tuweelah
I need to turn off the lights early tonight
Ana abi asakkir al layt badree fil layl
We want to stop here
Ehna nabi nwagef hne
We are from Mesaieed
Ehna men Mesaieed
The same building
Nafs el-mabna
I want to ask permission to leave
Ana abi as'al lao agdar amshi / atla
Tell me again
Gul'li marah thanya

*In Qatari Arabic, *ashan* means "because," but also here in Qatari usage, it simply means "to" and "in order to."

To open - Yeftah
A bit, a little, a little bit – Shway shway
To pay - Yedfa'a
Once again - Marrah thanya
There isn't/ there aren't - Ma fi
Sister - Ukht
To hope - Yetmanna
To live (to exist) – Y'ish
To live (in a place) – Yasken
Nice to meet you - Fursah sa'ideh
Name - Ism
Last name - Ism il ailah / Ism al akhir
To return – Yirjaa'
The Gulf – Al Khalij
Door - Bab/bawwabah

I need to open the door for my sister
Ana ahtaj aftah il-bab le ukhti
I need to buy something
Ana ashtari shai
I want to meet your sisters
Abi ashoof ekhwatak
Nice to meet you, what is your name and your last name
Fursah sa'idih, sheno ismak w ism a'iltak/al akhir?
To hope for a little better
Yitmanna shwai akthar
I want to return to Qatar
Ana abi arjaa' 'le gatar
I want to live 100 years
Ana abi a'ish miya sanah
I need to return your book
Ana abi arajji'lak il-ktab
Why are you sad right now?
(M)Int laish za'alan al heen? (F) enti laish za'alaneh al heen?
There aren't any people here
Ma fi ai ahad henee
There isn't enough time to go to Dubai today
Ma fi wagt kifaya nrooh le dubai elyom

*This *isn't* a phrase book! The purpose of this book is *solely* to provide you with the tools to create *your own* sentences!

To begin / To start - Yibda'
Afternoon – Ba'ad el thuhr
To happen - Yseer
To order - Yutlub/yu'mur
To drink - Yishrab
Excuse me - Lau samaht/ min fathlek
Child - (M) Walad, (F)bint
To finish - Yikhallas
To help - Ysa'id
To smoke – Ydakkhin
To love – Yhib
Gulf Cooperation Council – Majlis al-ta'aiwun al-khaliji

This must happen today
Hai lazim yseer el yoom
Excuse me, my child is here with me as well
Lao samaht woldi ma'ai hne alheen
I love you
Ahibaech
I see you
Ana ashoofak
I need you at my side
Ana ahtajak yanbi/ehzaee
I need to begin soon in order to be able to finish before 3 o'clock in the afternoon
Ana ahtaj abda' badri ashan akhallis gabl issa'ah thalatha ba'd ithuhr
I need help
Ana ahtaj musa'ada
I don't want to smoke once again
Ana ma abi adakhin marrah thanya
I want to learn how to speak Arabic
Ana abi at'allam aish'lon atakallam Arabi
I want to work for the Gulf Cooperation Council
Ana abi ashtighil fe majilis el ta'awun el khaliji

*"To help" is *ysa'id*. However, "help!" is *Musa'ada* "I need help" or "I need rescue" / *ana Ahtaj musa'adah*
*The definition of *ashan* is "in order to."

To read – Yagrah
To write – Yaktib
To teach - Ydarris/ y'allim
To close - Ygffil
To choose - Yikhtar
To prefer - Yfathil
To put - Yhut
Less - Agal
Sun - Shams
Month - Shahr
I talk - Ana bgool / atakalam
Exact – Bidzabt

I need this book in order to learn how to read and write in the Arabic language in order to study in Qatar
Ana ahtaj hai el kitab, ashan abi at'allam ashlon egra wiktob arabi ashan adros fi gattar
I want to close the door of the house
Ana abi aggfil bab al bayt
I prefer to put the gift here
Ana afathiil ahot il- hadiyyah hne
I want to pay less than you for the dinner
Ana abi adfa' agal minnak lal'asha
I speak with the boy and the girl in French
Ana batakalam ma'a al walad wal bint bil faransi
There is sun outside today
Fe shams barra elyoum
Is it possible to know the exact date?
Mumkin a'aref bidzabt il-tarikh?
Where is the airport
Wein il matar
I want to sleep
Abi anam

*With the knowledge you've gained so far, now try to create your own sentences!

To exchange (*money*) – Sarf floos/tabdil 'omlah
To call - Yittasil
Brother - Akh
Dad - Baba/ aboy, yba
To sit - Ajlis
Together - Ma' ba'th
To change - Yghayyir/ (for person) yitghayyar
Of course/certainly - Tab'an/Akeed
Welcome – Ahlan
During - Khilal
Years - Sanawat
Sky - Sama
Up – Fug / fok
Down - Taht
Sorry - Asif
To follow - Yilhag
To the - Lal
Big – Kbeer
New – Ydeed / jadeed
Never / ever – Abadan

I don't want to exchange this money at the bank
Ana ma abi abaddil il-floos fil bank
I want to call my brother and my son today
Ana abi attasil b okhuy w woldi elyom
Of course I can come to the theatre, and I want to sit together with you and with your sister
Akid ana agdar aji al-masrah, w abi ag'ud ma'ak w ma'a ukhtak
I need to go down to see your new house
Ana abi anzil ashan ashuf baitak al-yadeed/jadeed
I can see the sky from the window
Ana agdar ashuf issama min il- dareesha
I am sorry, but he wants to follow her to the store
Ana assif, bas hu yabi yilhagha lel-mahal
I don't ever want to see you
Ana ma abi ashufak marra thania

*In Qatari Arabic, "brother" is *akh*, and "dad" is *ab* However, "my dad" is *aboy*, and "my brother" is *akhuy*. "My sister" is *ukhti*, and "my mother" is *ommi*.
*In the English language the verb "to go down" isn't commonly used. However, in many foreign languages, the use of this verb is quite prevalent.
*For the possessive pronouns, her (*ha*) and him (*a*), both become suffixes to the verb or noun. Concerning nouns: her house / *bait'ha*, his house / *bata*. Concerning cases regarding verbs, please see page 19.

To allow - Yismah
To believe - Yisaddeg
Morning – Subh
Except – Illa
To promise - Yew'id
Good night - Tisbah ala khair
To recognize - Yit'arraf
People - Nas
Far - B'eed
Different - Gher
Man - Rayyal
To enter – Yidkhul
To receive - Yistalim
Pleasant – Ywenes / mutawad
Good afternoon - Masa'a-il-Khair
Left / right - Yasar, Yameen
Him / her - Hu / He
To move (an object) - Yharrik
To move (to a place) – Yintgil
Qatar – Qatar / Gatar

I need to allow him to go with us, he is a different man now
Ana abi asmahlu yiji ma'na, le'anna tghayyar el heen w-sar rayyal
I believe everything except this
Ana basadig kel illa hai ash'shay
I need to move the car because my sister needs to return home
Ana ahtaj aharek el sayarah ashan okhti tabi trjaa' al bayt
The people from Qatar are very pleasant
Al gatariieen wa'id mutawadieen
I need to find another hotel very quickly
Ana ahtaj alagey fundug thani besora'a
They need to receive a book for work
Hum yahtajoon yestlmoon ketab lel amal
I see the sun in the morning
Ana ashoof el shames fe as'subh
The house is on the other end of the street
Il-bait mawjud fi nehayat ash'shareh

To wish - Yitmanna
Bad – Mo zain
To get - Yakhud
To forget - Yinsa
Past – Zaman, Mathi
Everybody / Everyone - Kul wahad/ il-kul
To feel - Yhis
Although - Raghim
Next (following, after) - Illy-ba'du/ (next time) ilmarrah-ijjay
To like – Yhib
In front - Giddam
Next (near, close) - Gareeb / janb
Behind – Wara
Well (as in doing well) - Zain
Restaurant - Mat'am
Bathroom – Hammam
Goodbye - Ma' issalamah

I don't want to wish you anything bad
Ana ma abi atmannalek ay shi mob zain
I must forget everybody from my past in order to feel well
Ana lazem ansa kol wahed men el mathi ashan agdar akoon zain
I am next to the person behind you
Ana janb el shakis ele warak
There is a person in front of me
Fe shakis gedammy
Goodbye my friends
Ma assalamah ya asdiqai
Where is the bathroom in the restaurant?
Wain Il-hammam fil-mat'am?
She has to buy a car before the next year
Hiyya lazem tashteri sayyarah gabl il-sanah el jaiya
I like the house, but it is very small
Ana habait al bayt, bus kathir sagheer

To remove / to take out - Yishil
Please - Law samaht
Beautiful - Jamil (M) / Jamilah (F)
To lift - Yirfa'a
Correct – Sah / Sahih
Belong - Milk
To hold - Yimsik, yitmassak
To check - Yifhas
Small - Sgheer
Real - Hagege
Weather - Ijjaw
Size - Hajm
High – A'aali
So (as in then) - Ashan, ya'ani
Price - Si'r
So (as in very) - Kilosh
Diamond – Almas

She wants to remove this door please
Heya tabi tshil el bab Lao samaht
This week the weather was very beautiful
Hai el osboo'a al jaw kan killosh zain
I need to know which is the real diamond
Ana lazim a'rif el almas al hagege
We need to know the size of the house
Lazim na'rif hajm al bayt
I want to lift this, so you need to hold it high
Ana abi arfaa' hai, ashan lazim tarf'aha a'li
I can pay this even though that the price is so expensive
Ana agdar adfa' hai ma'a eno el se'aer kilosh ghali
Is this price correct?
Hai el sa'aer sahih?

*In Qatari Arabic, *il-se'r* means "the amount."

*In Arabic, the articles "this" and "that" become reversed when preceding a noun. "This" (hai) "week" *(usbu'u)* becomes *thak il-'usbu'u*.

**Fatoorah* means "bill."

Building Bridges

In Building Bridges, we take six conjugated verbs that have been selected after studies I have conducted for several months in order to determine which verbs are most commonly conjugated into first person. For example, once you know how to say, "I need," "I want," "I can," and "I like," you will be able to connect words and say almost anything you want more correctly and understandably. The following contain these six conjugated verbs in first, second, third, fourth, and fifth person, as well as some sample sentences. Please master the entire program up until here prior to venturing onto this section.

I want - Ana abi
I need - Ana ahtaj
I can - Ana agdar
I like - Ana bi'jibni, ana bahib
I go - Ana aruh
I have - Ana indi
I must / I have to - Ana lazim

I can go with you to the bus station
Ana agdar arooh ma'ek le mahatet el bas
I need to walk to the museum
Ana lazim amshi lil mut-haf
I like to ride the train
Ana ahib arkab il-gitar
I have to speak to my teacher
Ana lazim atakallam ma'a estathi
I have a book
Ana indi ktab

Please master *every* single up until here prior to attempting the following!

You want / do you want – Tabi / enta tabi?
He wants / does he want - Huwa yabi / Huwa yabi?
She wants / does she want - Hiya tabi / Hiya tabi?
We want / do we want - Ihna nabi / Ihna nabi?
They want / do they want - Hum yaboon / Hum yaboon?
You (plural) want / do you need - Antum taboon / Antum taboon?

You need / do you need - Int tahtaj / int tahtaj?
He needs / does he need – Huwwa Yahtaj / Huwwa Yahtaj?
She needs / does she need – Heya Tahtaj / Heya Tahtaj?
We need / do we need - Ehna Nahtaj / Ehna Nahtaj?
They need / do they need - Hum Yahtajoon / Hum Yahtajoon?
You (plural) need/ do you need? - Intu Tahtajoon / intu Tahtajoon?

You can / can you - Inta Tagdar / Inta Tagdar?
He can / can he - Yagdar / Yagdar?
She can / can she - Heya Tagdar / Heya Tagdar?
We can / can we - Ihna Nagdar / Ihna Nagdar?
They can / can they - Yagdaroon / Yagdaroon?
You (plural) can - Antum Tagdaroon / Antum Tagdaroon?

You like / do you like – Int Tahib / Int Tahib?
He likes / does he like –Yahib / Yahib?
She like / does she like –Tahib / Tahib?
We like / do we like – Ihna Nahib / Ihna i'jibna?
They like / do they like - Hum Yahiboon / Hum I'jiboon?
You (plural) like – Ento Tahiboon / Ento Tahiboon?

You go / do you go - Int Taruh / int Taruh?
He goes / does he go - Yaruh / Yaruh?
She goes / does she go - Taruh / Taruh?
We go / do we go - Ihna Naruh / ihna Naruh?
They go / do they go –Yaruhoon / Yaruhoon?
You (plural) go/ do you go – Intu Taruhoon / Intu Taruhoon?
You have / do you have – Int indak/ Int indak?
He has / does he have –Inda / Inda?
She has / does she have –Indaha / Indaha?
We have / do we have – Ihna indna/ Ihna indna?
They have / do they have –Induhom / Induhom?
You (plural) have/ do you have – Antum indokum / Antum indokum?

*Keep in mind in some cases the pronoun isn't required to precede the verb. For example "you want" *int tigdar*, you can simply just say *tagdar*.

Do you want to go?
Inta tabi tetla'a

Does he want to fly?
Huwwa Yabi yteer?

We want to swim
Hnna Nabi nisbah

Do they want to run?
Hum yaboon yerkthoon?

Do you need to clean?
Ente Tahtaj tunathif?

She needs to sing a song
Heyya lazim tgha'ani ghnya

We need to travel
Hnna lazim nsafer

They don't need to fight
Hum mob lazim yat'hawashoon

You (plural) need to see
Intum lazim tashufoon / tatafarrajoon

Can you hear me?
Enta tegdar tesma'any

Yes, he can dance very well
Ay howa yegdar yergos zain

We can go out tonight
Nehna negdar netla'a el Laylah

They can break the wood
Hum yegdaro yeksaro el khashab

Do you like to eat here?
Enta teheb takol hne?

He likes to spend time here
Huwa yahib yamdi el wagt hne

We like to fix the house
Hena nheb nsaleh el bayt

They like to cook
Hum yheboon yetbakhoon

You (plural) like my house?
Antum a'ajibkum bayti?

Do you go to school today?
Int rayih al-madrasah elyom?

He goes fishing
Huwa rayih yseed samak

We are going to relax
Ehna ha nastarkhi

They go to watch a film
Hum rayhin yitafarrajoon film

Do you have money?
Int ma'ak floos?

She must look outside
Heya Lazim tshuf barra

We have to sign our names
Hena lazim nwaggi' asamina

They have to send the letter
Hum lazim ywaddo il- risalah

You (plural) have to order
Antum lazim tatlubo

Countries of the Middle East

Dowal il-sharq il-awsat
Lebanon - Lubnan
Syria - Surya
Jordan - Il-urdun
Saudi Arabia - Il-Suudiyah
Israel/Palestine/West Bank - Isra'il/Falastin/il-diffih il-gharbiyyih
Bahrain - Il-Bahrain
Yemen - Yaman
Oman - Uman
United Arab Emirates - Il-Imarat
Kuwait - Il-Kuwait
Iraq - Il- Iraq
Qatar - Qatar
Morocco - Il-Maghrib
Algeria - Il-jaza'ir
Libya - Libya
Egypt - Masir
Tunisia - Tunis

Months
January – Kanun il-thani
February - Shbat
March - Athar
April - Nisan
May - Ayyar
June - Huzayran
July - Tammuz
August - Aab
September - Aylul
October - Tishreen awwal
November- Tishreen thani
December - Kanun awwal

Days of the Week
Sunday - Yum il-ahad
Monday - Yum il-ithnin
Tuesday - Yum il-thulatha'
Wednesday - Yum al-'arbi'aa
Thursday - Yum il-khamees
Friday - Yum il-jom'a
Saturday - Yum issabt

Seasons
Spring - Rabee'
Summer - Saif
Autumn - Khareef
Winter - Shita

Cardinal Directions
North - Shamal
South – Janoob
East - Sharq
West – Gharb

Colors
Black - (M)Aswad (F) Sawda
White - (M)Abyad (F)Baida
Gray - (M)Ramadi (F) Ramadiyyah
Red - (M)Ahmar (F)Hamra
Blue - (M)Azrag (F)Zarga
Yellow - (M)Asfar (F)Safra
Green - (M)Akhdar (F)Khadra
Orange - (M)Burtuqali/(F) Burtugaliyyah
Purple - Banafsaj (M) Banafsajiyyah (F)
Brown - (M)Bunni (F) Bunniyyah

Numbers
One – Wahid
Two – Ithnain
Three – Thalatha
Four - Arba'ah
Five – Khamsah
Six – Sittah
Seven - Sab'ah
Eight – Thamaniyah
Nine - Tis'ah
Ten - 'Asharah
Twenty - 'Ishreen
Thirty - Talateen
Forty - Arb'in
Fifty - Khamseen
Sixty - Sitteen
Seventy - Sab'een
Eighty - Tamaneen
Ninety - Tis'een
Hundred – Emiyah
Thousand - Alf
Million - Malyun

Conversational
Arabic Quick
and easy

KUWAITI DIALECT

YATIR NITZANY

THE KUWAITI DIALECT

As in many other Arabic countries, Modern Standard Arabic (MSA) is taught alongside the local dialects in Kuwait. Modern Standard Arabic is the official language of Kuwait, but Kuwaiti Arabic is the urban spoken vernacular used in everyday life in the country. There are differences between the dialects spoken in urban areas and those spoken in rural areas.

MSA is used for instruction in state and private schools and at universities. It is also used for documents, magazines, books, and newspapers.

Kuwaiti Arabic features loan words from Indian, English, Persian, Turkish, and Italian due to trade and immigration. Kuwaiti Arabic is locally known as Khaliji, and as Khamseh and Al Hasaa in other Arab nations. Kuwaiti Arabic shares many phonetic features unique to Gulf dialects. Due to Kuwait's soap opera industry, Kuwaiti Arabic spread throughout the Arabic-speaking world and became familiar even to people in countries such as Tunisia and Jordan.

The total number of speakers of Kuwaiti Arabic is around 1.3 million.

There have been dramatic changes in the lifestyle and occupations of the people of Kuwait and these have had implications for their language. For example, the replacement of maritime occupations following the discovery of oil has had dramatic implications on the vocabulary of Kuwaiti Arabic. Globalization is also providing an impact on Kuwaiti Arabic. For example, the use of English as a language in certain areas of life and various contacts with other, non-Arabic, community languages.

Spoken in: Kuwait and other Gulf States

ARABIC PRONUNCIATIONS

PLEASE MASTER THE FOLLOWING PAGE IN ARABIC PRONUNCIATIONS PRIOR TO STARTING THE PROGRAM

Kha. For Middle Eastern languages including Arabic, Hebrew, Farsi, Pashto, Urdu, Hindi, etc., and also German, to properly pronounce the kh or ch is essential, for example, *Khaled* (a Muslim name) or *Chanukah* (a Jewish holiday) or *Nacht* ("night" in German). The best way to describe kh or ch is to say "ka" or "ha" while at the same time putting your tongue at the back of your throat and blowing air. It's pronounced similarly to the sound that you make when clearing your throat. Please remember this whenever you come across any word containing a kh in this program.

Ghayin. The Arabic gh is equivalent to the "g" in English, but its pronunciation more closely resembles the French "r," rather than "g." Pronounce it at the back of your throat. The sound is equivalent to what you would make when gargling water. Gha is pronounced more as "rha," rather than as "ga." *Ghada* is pronounced as "rhada." In this program, the symbol for *ghayin* is gh, so keep your eyes peeled.

Aayin is pronounced as a'a, pronounced deep at the back of your throat. Rather similar to the sound one would make when gagging. In the program, the symbol for *aayin* is *a'a, u'u, o'o,* or *i'i.*

Ha is pronounced as "ha." Pronunciation takes place deep at the back of your throat, and for correct pronunciation, one must constrict the back of the throat and exhale air while simultaneously saying "ha." In the program, this strong h ("ha") is emphasized whenever *ha, ah, hi, he,* or *hu* is encountered.

NOTE TO THE READER

The purpose of this book is merely to enable you to communicate in the Kuwaiti Arabic dialect. In the program itself (pages 17-38) you may notice that the composition of some of those sentences might sound rather clumsy. This is intentional. These sentences were formulated in a specific way to serve two purposes: to facilitate the easy memorization of the vocabulary and to teach you how to combine the words in order to form your own sentences for quick and easy communication, rather than making complete literal sense in the English language. So keep in mind that this is not a phrase book!

As the title suggests, the sole purpose of this program is for conversational use only. It is based on the mirror translation technique. These sentences, as well as the translations are not incorrect, just a little clumsy. Latin languages, Semitic languages, and Anglo-Germanic languages, as well as a few others, are compatible with the mirror translation technique.

Many users say that this method surpasses any other known language learning technique that is currently out there on the market. Just stick with the program and you will achieve wonders!

Note to the Reader

Again, I wish to stress this program is by no means, shape, or form a phrase book! The sole purpose of this book is to give you a fundamental platform to enable you to connect certain words to become conversational. Please also read the "Introduction" and the "About Me" section prior to commencing the program.

In order to succeed with my method, please start on the very first page of the program and fully master one page at a time prior to proceeding to the next. Otherwise, you will overwhelm yourself and fail. Please do not skip pages, nor start from the middle of the book.

It is a myth that certain people are born with the talent to learn a language, and this book disproves that myth. With this method, anyone can learn a foreign language as long as he or she follows these explicit directions:

* Memorize the vocabulary on each page

* Follow that memorization by using a notecard to cover the words you have just memorized and test yourself.

* Then read the sentences following that are created from the vocabulary bank that you just mastered.

* Once fully memorized, give yourself the green light to proceed to the next page.

Again, if you proceed to the following page without mastering the previous, you are guaranteed to gain nothing from this book. If you follow the prescribed steps, you will realize just how effective and simplistic this method is.

The Program
Let's Begin! "Vocabulary" (Memorize the Vocabulary)

I | I am – Ana
With you – **(M)** Wayak/Ma'ak / **(Fem)** Wyach/Ma'ach
With him / with her - **(M)** Wayah/ Maah **(F)** Wyaha/ Maaha
With us – Way'aana
For you - Ashanik
Without him – Bedona/Mo Maah
Without them - Bedonhom/Mo Maahom
Always - Daimaan
Was – Kan
This, this is - **(M)** Haathaak / **(F)** Hathiik/ **(Neuter)** Hatha
Is, it's, it is - Hatha
Sometimes – 'Marat o Marat'/Sa'at
Maybe – Yemkin
You / you are / are you – (M) Inta / (F) Inty
You plural - Into
Is it - (M) Wohowa (F) Wehyi
Today – Elyoum
Better – Ahsan
He / he is - Ohwa
She / she is – Ehya
From - Min
from where – Min wain?

Sentences composed from the vocabulary

This is for you
Hatha Ashanik (M)/Ashanich (F)
I am from Kuwait
Ana min el-kuwait
Are you from Kuwait?
Inta min el-kuwait?
I am with you
Ana wayak(M)/ wayach (F)
Sometimes you are with us at the mall
Awgaat enta way'aana fel soog
I am always with her
Ana daiman wayaha/ma'aha.
Are you without them today?
Inta mo wayahom/ma'ahom elyoum? **Sometimes I am with him** Awgaat/sa'at Ana wayah/ma'ah.

---

*In Kuwaiti Arabic, there are gender rules. Saying "for you" to a male is *ashanik* but if you are talking to a female, it's *ashanich*.

*To indicate "with him"/ "with her," we use (M) *wayah* / (F) *wayaha*.

*In Kuwaiti Arabic, "with you" is *wayak, wayachi*; however, *ma' baa'th* may be used as well. *Ma' baa'th* is basically an expression used to indicate "we are together."

I was - Ana Kint
To be - **(M)** Ykun / **(F)** Tkun
The - El / Al
Same – Nafs/Methel
Good - Zayn
Here - Hne
Very / much – Wayed
And - Wa
Between - Bain
Now – Elheen
Later / after / afterwards - Ba'adeen/Ogob
If – Law, Ithaa
Yes – Ee
To – Hag
Tomorrow – Bacher
You - (M) Enta / (F) Enti
Also / too / as well – Baad

If it's between now and later
Itha kan bain elhen o baadeen.
It's better tomorrow
Ahsan bacher
This is good as well
Heta hatha zain
To be the same person
(M)Ykun/(F) Tkun nafs el-shakhs
Yes, you are very good
Ee, inta wayed zain
I was here with them
Ana kent mne/hne maahom
You and I
Enta o ana.
The same day
Nafs elyoum

The Program

Me – Li/ Hagy
Ok – Mashy/Tamam
Even if - Hatta law / Etha
No – Laa / Mo Saheeh
Worse - Aswa'
Where – Wain
Everything – Kel shay
Somewhere - Eb Mokan
What - Shenu?
Almost - Tagriban
There – Hnak

Afterwards is worse
Ba'adeen aswa'
Even if I go now
Hatta law bnrooh Alheen
Where is everything?
Wain Kel shay?
Maybe somewhere
Yimken eb mokan
What? I am almost there
Sheno? Ana tagreban Menak/Hnak
Where are you?
(M) Enta wein? / (F) Enti wein?
Where is the airport?
Wain el-matar?
Where is the embassy
Wain el-qonsolya/Wain el-safara?

*"There" has two meanings, so it is *Hnak/Mnak* (Just different pronunciation), depending on the context. When we say "there is" we say *yojad/fe* / but when we say "I am there" (place) we say *ana hnak*.
* *Eb Mokan* literally means "in a place."
* In Arabic, the pronoun "me" has several definitions. In relation to verbs, it's *li/hagy Li/hagy* refers to any verb that relates to the action of doing something to someone or for someone.
For example, "tell me," "tell (to) me" / *(M) gool li*.
ana just means "me": "love me" / *Hobany Ana*
Other variations (*ya*):
   * "on me" / *'alaai*
   * "in me" / *Feny*
   * "to me" / *Hagy*
   * "with me" / *wayay*
The same rule applies for "him" and "her"—both become suffixes: –*o* and –*a*.
Basically all verbs pertinent to male end with *h*, and all pertinent to female end with *a*.
* "love her" / *Ahebha*
* "love him" / *Aheba*
* "love them" / *Ahebhom*
* "love us" / *hebbna*
Any verb that relates to doing someone to someone, for someone put *l*:
* "tell her" / *gool-lha*
* "tell him" / *gool-lah*
* "tell them" / *gool-lhom*
* "tell us" / *ygool-lna/ygool- hagna*
Adding you as a suffix in Arabic is *ak* or *lak,* female *lich*.
* "love you" /(M) *Ahebak* / (F) *Ahebech* /"tell you" / (M) *Agoolak*/ (F) *Agoolich*

House - Bait
In / at - Fe / Fel
Car – Sayara
Already – Asasan
Good morning - Sabah el kheir
How are you? – (M) Shlonek/ (F) Shlonech
Where are you from? – (M) Enta min wain/(F) Enty min wain?
Today - El-youm
Hello – Hayaak allah/'Ahlan o sahlan'
What is your name? – (M) Sheno esmik/ (F) Sheno esmich
How old are you? –Cham Omrak?
Son –Walad
Daughter - Bint
To have – (M) Enda/ (F) 'Endaha / (self) 'Endy
Doesn't –Mo
Hard – Sa'eb
Still – Lay-alhen
Then (or "so") – Ba'adeen/ Ya'any

She doesn't have a car, so maybe she is still at the house?
Ehya ma Endaha sayara, Fa momoken (or Yemkin) Ehya Lay-alheen fe Al-bait
I am in the car already with your son and daughter
Ana fe El-sayara assasan Ma'a wildek o bintik
Good morning, how are you today?
Sabah el kheir,(M) shlonak (F) Shlonech el-youm?
Hello, what is your name?
Hayaak allah/Ahlan/Slam, shenu esmak?
How old are you?
Cham Omrak?
This is very hard, but it's not impossible
Hatha wayed sa'ab, bas mo mostahel
Then where are you from?
Ael enta min wain?

*In Arabic, possessive pronouns become suffixes to the noun. For example, in the translation for "your," *ek* is the masculine form, and *ch* is the feminine form.
- "Your book" / *Ketabek*(m.) *Ketabich* (f.) / "Your house" / *Baitek* (m.), *baititsh* (f.).

* In Kuwaiti Arabic, in the event that "doesn't" is used regarding negations of verbs, the following requirements must precede and follow *Mo ... ash*, for example: "she doesn't like the orange juice" (The verb "like" is *Ehib*) –*Ehya ma t-hib asser el-bortogal*.

The Program

Thank you – Mashkour/Shokran
For - Hag
Anything - Ay shay
That / That is – (M) Thak/(F) Thik
Time - Wagt/Sa'ah
But – Bas
No / not – Mo / La'
I am not - Ana Mo
Away – B'eed
Late - Mit'akher
Similar – Nafs / Mithl
Another/ other - Thani
Side – Janb
Until - Lahad
Yesterday – Ams
Without us – Bedona
Since - Men
Day - Youm
Before – Gabl

Thanks for everything
Mashkour 'ala Kel shay
It's almost time
Hathi tagreban el sa'a
I am not here, I am away
Ana mo Hne, Ana baeed.
That is a similar house
Hatha nafs/methel/yshabih el-bait
I am from the other side
Ana min el-soob el-thani
But I was here until late yesterday
Bas ana kent meny layen ams bel-lail.
I am not at the other house
Ana mo fe/eb el-bait el-thani

.

*In Kuwaiti Arabic, with negations such as "no," "not," "doesn't," "can't," and "don't," use either *Mo* or *la*. *La* is used to indicate cases such as "are you here" – e*nta Hny* – and you then reply "no," *la*. *Mo* is used to indicate cases of "not," "doesn't," or "don't," for example: "I am not at the other house" is *Ana mo fe el-bait el-thani*. In some instances both cases of *la* and *Mo* may be used, for example; "can you come?" "No, I can't," *La Ma Agder*.

*In Kuwaiti Arabic, there are three definitions for time:
*"Time" / *wagt* refers to "era", "moment period," "duration of time."
*"Time(s)" / *marra(t)/sa'at* refers to "occasion" or "frequency."
*"Time" / *sa'a* references "hour," "what time is it?"

What time is it? - Sa'a cham?
I say / I am saying – Bgool
I want - Ana Aby
Without you – (M) Bdonek /(F) Bdonech
Everywhere /wherever –Kel makan
I go - Barooh
With - Ma'
My – Li
Cousin (paternal) - (M) Wald 'amy / (F) Bent 'amy / (P) (M) Wlaad 'amy
Cousin (maternal) - (M) Wald khaly / (F) Bent khali / (P)(M) Wlaad khaly / (P)(F) Banat khaly
I need - Mehtag/Ahtag
Right now –Elheen
Night – Lail
To see – shoof
Light – Noor/Lait
Outside –Barah
Without - Bedon
Happy - Sa'eed/Mestanes
I see / I am seeing – Shayef/Ashoof

I am saying no / I say no
Ana Agol la/ Ana gelt la
I want to see this today
Ana aby ashoof hatha el-yom
I am with you everywhere
Ana ma'ak eb kel mokan
I am happy without any cousins here
Ana mestanis bedon ay eayal am.
I need to be there at night
Ana Lazem akon menak belail.
I see light outside
Ana ashoof laitat(P)or Lait(S) barah
What time is it right now?
Esa'ah cham el'heen?

*"Mine" / *li* is also a possessive pronoun. *Li* means "my" but also becomes a suffix to a noun. Nouns ending in a vowel end with –*teh*. Nouns ending with a consonant end with –*y*. For example:
   * "cousin" / *Eayal elam*, "my cousin" / *walad/Eayal amy*
   * "cup" / *koob*, "my cup" / *kooby*

For second and third person masculine noun, *walad* ("son"), male (S) *ak*, (P) *kom* female (S) *ik*, (P) *kum*. "His" –*haga* / "hers" – *hagha* noun endings will be *o* (for male) and *a* (for female).
   * "your son" / *weldik* (m.), *weldich* (f.), "your (plural) son" / *weldokom* (m.), *bintkom* (f.), "his son" / *welda* , "her son" / *weldha*, "our son" / *waladna*
   * "their son" / *wldhom*

For second and third person feminine noun: "car" / *sayara*.
   * "your car" / *sayartek*, "your (plural) car" / *sayaretkom*
   * "his car" / *sayarta*, "her car" / *sayaret-ha*
   * "our car" / *sayaretna*, "their car" / *sayarthom*

*This *isn't* a phrase book! The purpose of this book is *solely* to provide you with the tools to create *your own* sentences!

The Program

Place – Mokan
Easy - Sahil
To find - Yilga
To look for / to search – Fattish
Near / Close - Gareeb
To wait – Yanter
To sell - (M) Ybee' - (F) Tbee' / (To be sold) - Tenbaa'/Yenbaa'
To use - Yestakhdim
To know – Y'arif
To decide – Ygarir
Between - Bainn
Both – Elthnain
To – Hag

This place it's easy to find
Hatha elmakan sahil ylgaah
I want to look for this next to the car
Aby alga hatha yam/janb el-sayara.
I am saying to wait until tomorrow
Ana agool enter lain bacher.
This table is easy to sell (to be sold)
Hathi eltawla sahil tenbaa'
I want to use this
Aby astamel/astakdem hatha.
I need to know where (location) is the house
Ahtag aaref wain mokan el-bait.
I want to decide between both places
Aby agarir bain el-mokanain
I need to find the hospital
Ahtag alagy el-mostashfa.

*In Kuwaiti Arabic, to indicate "to," *Hag* may be used. *La* is placed preceding a noun. In a phrase such as "going to a place," for instance, *Hag* is used to precede a verb, or to indicate "In order to." In certain instances, *la* may be used, for example: "in order to go to Kuwait City," *Ashan nrooh hag madinat el-kuwait.*

*In Kuwaiti Arabic, "to sell" is (M) *ybee'* / (F) *tbee'* For "to be sold," however, we use *tenbaa/yenbaa'*.

Because – Ashan
To buy – Yeshteri
They – Ohma
Bottle – Botal
Beach – Bahar
Book - Kitab
Mine – Li
To understand - Yifham
Problem / Problems - (S) Mushkilah / (P) Mashakil
I do / I am doing – Asawy
Of - Men
To look – Yitfaggad
Myself - Nafsi
Enough - Kefaya / Kaafi
Food / water - Akl / May
Each/ every/ entire/ all – Koll
Hotel - Fondog

I like this hotel because I want to look at the beach
Ana aheb hatha el-fondog ashan ana abi ashoof elbahar.
I want to buy a bottle of water
Aby ashtry botol may.
I do this every day
Ana asawy hatha kill youm
Both of them have enough food
El-ethnein 'andohom akl kefaya O ykafehom
That is the book, and that book is mine
Hatha huwa l-ktab, w hathaa el-ktab Hagy
I need to understand the problem
Ahtag a'aref/afham el-moshkela
I see the view of the city from the hotel
Ashoof el-view/elmanthar mal el-madina min el-fondog
I do my homework today
Ana Asawy wajebaty elyoum
My entire life (*all my life*)
Kol hayaty

*"Both of them" is *el-ethnein*

The Program

I like – Ana aheb
There is / There are – Fee / Yojad
Family / Parents - 'Ayleh / Walidin
Why – Laish
To say – Ygool
Something - Shay
To go – (M) Yimshy / (F) Timshy
Ready – Jahiz
Soon - Gareeban
To work – Eldawam
Who – Meno
To know – Ye'rif
That (conjunction) – Inno / law

I like to be at my house with my parents
Ana aheb akon bel-bait ma'a ahaly.
I want to know why I need to say something important
Aby a'aref laish lazem agool shay mohem
I am there with him
Ana hnak ma'a
I am busy, but I need to be ready soon
Ana mashgool, bass ahtag akoon jahiz gareeban
I like to go to work
Ana Aheb arooh ashtogol
'Who is there?
Meno henak?
I want to know if they are here, because I want to go outside
Aby a'aref etha ohma menak, ashan aby arooh bara
There are seven dolls
Hnak fee sab'at al'ab
I need to know that it is a good idea
Ana Ahtag aaref ena hathy elfekra zainah

*In the last sentence, we use "that" as a conjunction (*inna*) and a demonstrative pronoun *(M) Hatha / (F) Hathi)*.
*In Kuwaiti Arabic, "to work" is *eldawam* however *nikhdm* or may be used as well. To work (as in to do work) is *nikhdim*. However to work (at a job) is *eldawam*. "I am going to work in the garden" - *ana rah ashtigel fe elhadega,* however "I'm going to work (job)" - *ana rayeh El- dawam.*

How much /How many – Cham
To bring – Yijeeb
With me - Wayaya
Instead - Badal
Only - Bass
When – Lama / Miita
Or – Aw
I can / Can I – Ana egdar / Egdar
Were - Kan
Without me – Mo wayaya
Fast – Saree'
Slow –batee'
Cold – Bard
Inside –Dakel
To eat – Yakol
Hot –Haar
To Drive – Ysoog

How much money do I need to bring with me?
Cham floos ahtag ashan ayeb ma'ay?
Instead of this cake, I want that cake
Badal thik el kaike, aby hathi elkayka
Only when you can
Bas lama tegdar
They were without me yesterday
Ohmah ma kano may ams
Do I need to drive the car fast or slow?
Hal ahtag asoog elsayara sary' aw batee'?
It is cold inside the library
Bard Dakel el-maktabeh
Yes, I like to eat this hot for my lunch
Ee, ana aheb akel hatha haar hag elgada.
I can work today
Egdar arooh el dawam el-youm

*"Were" is *kan*, but for "they were," "We were" is Kena

*"I can" and "can I?" is *egdar/ ana egdar*. "You can" or "can you?" is *tegdar?*

The Program

To answer (the phone) – Yredd
To answer (a question) - Yjeeb/Yredd
To fly - Yteer
Time / Times - Marra / Marrat
To travel – Ysafer
To learn - (M) Yt'alam / (F) Tet'alam
How – Shlon
To swim – (M) Yesbah / (F) Tesbah
To practice - Yitmaran
To play – Yel'aab
To leave – Yitrok/Ykaly
Many /much /a lot – Wayed
I go to - Brooh
First - Awal
Time / Times – Marra/Marrat

I want to answer many questions
Ana aby ajaweb wayed as'ila.
I must fly to Dubai today
Ana lazem ateer hag Dubai elyoum
I need to learn how to swim at the pool
Ana ahtag ata'lam shloon asbah fe hmmam elsebaha
I want to learn to play better tennis
Ana aby ata'lam alab tennis ahsan
I want to leave this here for you when I go to travel the world
Ana aby akaly hatha hne hagach laman arooh asafer elalam
Since the first time
Men awel marra
The children are yours
Elawlad ilak

*In Kuwaiti Arabic, "to answer", as in "answer the phone," is *Yredd*; to answer a question it is *yjaweb*.

*In Kuwaiti Arabic, "to leave (something)" is *ykaly* "To leave (a place)" is *yimmshy*.

*In Kuwaiti Arabic, there are three definitions for time:
   - "Time" / *wagt* refers to "era", "moment period," "duration of time."
   - "Time(s)" / *marra(t)* refers to "occasion" or "frequency."
   - "Time" / *sa'a* references "hour," "what time is it?"

***With the knowledge you've gained so far, now try to create your own sentences!**

Nobody / Anyone – 'walah ahad'
Against - Dedd
Us – Ehna
To visit - Yizoor
Mom / Mother – Om / Yomma
To give – Yaty
Which - Ay
To meet - Yiltigy
Someone – Wahad
Just - Bass
To walk – Yitmasha
Around – Hawl
Towards - Bitijaah
Than - Min
Nothing – 'wala shay'

Something is better than nothing
Shay afdal min wala shay
I am against him
Ana Deda
Is there anyone here?
Fi ay ahad hne/mny?
We go to visit my family each week
Ehna nrooh nzoor al-ahal kell esbooa'.
I need to give you something
Ana ahtag aatek shay
Do you want to go meet someone?
Taby tshoof ahad?
I was here on Wednesdays as well
Ana kent hne el-arbea'a baad
Do you do this every day?
Ente tsawy hatha kell youm?
You need to walk around, but not towards the house
Enta tehtag temshy, bas mo bitijah el bait

*In Arabic, when using the pronoun "you" as a direct and indirect object pronoun (the person who is actually affected by the action that is being carried out) in relation to a verb, the pronoun "you" becomes a suffix to that verb. That suffix becomes *ek* (masc.) *ich*(fem.).
   * "to give" / *yaty*: "to give you" / *yateek*
   * "to tell" / *ygool*: "to tell you" / *ygoolek* (m.), *ygoolich* (f.)
   * "see you" /*yshoofek* "to see you" (plural) / *yshofoonik* (m.), *yshofoonech* (f.)
For third person male, add *o* and *on* for plural, for female add *a* and *on* for plural.
   * "tell him" / *ygoola*
   * "tell her" / *ygoolha*
   * "see them" / *shofohom* (m.), *shofohom* (f.)
   * "see us " /*shoofona*

The Program

I have – 'Andy
Don't – Ma
Friend – Rab' / Sadeeg
To borrow – Yesta'eer
To look like / resemble – Yishbah
Like (preposition) – Nafs / methel
Grandfather – Yadd
To want – taby (f) yaby (M)
To stay – ygaad
To continue - Yikamil
Way – Tareeg
I don't - ana ma
To show - Yewarri
To prepare - Yehaddir
I am not going - 'Aani mo rayeh

Do you want to look like Salim
Taby tseer methel shakel Salim
I want to borrow this book for my grandfather
Ana aby aastaeer hatha elketab hag yaddy.
I want to drive and to continue on this way to my house
Ana aby asoog o astmir ala hatha el-tareq lay baity
I have a friend there, that's why I want to stay in Al Ahmadi
Ana endy rabe' hne, ashan chethy ana aby agad fee al-ahmadi
I am not going to see anyone here
Ana ma rah ahoof ahad mne
I need to show you how to prepare breakfast
Ana ahtag awareek shloon t-hather elryoog
Why don't you have the book?
Leish ma indak l-ktab?
That is incorrect, I don't need the car today
Hatha mo saheh, ana mo mehtag l-sayara l-youm

* "he wants" / *howa dayer*
* "she wants" / *heiya dayra*

To remember – Yet-thakkar
Dark/Darkness – Thalaam/Tholoomat
Your – (M) Lik/ (F) lich
Number - Ragm
Hour - Sa'aa
About / On the - 'Ala / 'Ala el
Grandmother - Yadda
Five - Khamsa
Minute / minutes – Dgeega / Dgayeg
More - Akthar
To think – Yifakker
To do – Ydeer
To come – Yijjy
To hear – Yesma'
Last – Akher

You need to remember my number
Enta/enti tehtag tet-thakkar ragmy
This is the last hour of darkness
Hathy akher Sa'aa min el tholomaat
I want to come and to hear my grandmother speak Arabic
Ana aby ajy/aye o asma' yadety tetkalam bel 'araby
I need to think more about this, and what to do
Ana ahtag afker fe hatha akthar. O shno asawi
From here to there, it's only five minutes
Min hne lay hnak/mnak, bas khamsat dgayeg
The school on the mountain
L madrasa 'ala el jabal

The Program

To leave –Ytla'
Again - Marra thanya
To take - Yakhith
To try - Yijarrib
To rent – Yista'jjir
Without her – Mo maaha/Bedonha
We are – Ehna
To turn off - Yitfy
To ask – Yis'al
To stop - Yiwaggif
Permission - Ithn

He needs to leave and rent a house at the beach
Ohwa yhtag yrooh o yajer bait ala elbahar
I want to take the test without her
Ana aby akih el-emtihan bedonha
We are here a long time
Ehna hna wagt taweel
I need to turn off the lights early tonight
Ana ahtag ataffy el-laytat mbacher el-lailah
We want to stop here
Naby nwaggif hne
We are from Al Jehra
Ehna min el-jehra
The same building
Nafs el-benaye
I want to ask permission to leave
Ana aby is'aal 'ala ithn imshy
I want to sleep
ana aby 'naam

*In Kuwaiti Arabic, "to stop" is *ywaagif*, "to cease" is also *wagf*.

To open - Yiftah
A bit, a little, a little bit - Shway
To pay – Yidfa'
Once again – Marra thanya
There isn't/ there aren't – Ma fee
Sister - Ikht
To hope - Yitmanna
To live – Y'eesh
Nice to meet you – Etsharaft b ma'reftak
Name - Esm
Last name - Esm el 'ayla
To return – Yerjaa'
Door - Baab

I need to open the door for my sister
Ana ahtag aftah el-baab hag okaty
I need to buy something
Ana ahtag ashtry shay
I want to meet your sisters
Ana aby altagy oktak.
Nice to meet you, what is your name and your last name
Esharaft b ma'reftak, sheno esmak w esm 'eltak?
To hope for a little better
Yitmanna shway ahsan
I want to return from the United States and to live in Qatar without problems
Ana aby irjaa' min america w e'eesh fe Qatar mo waya mashakel
Why are you sad right now?
Laish enta zalaan elheen
There aren't any people here
Ma fe nas hne
There isn't enough time to go to Bubiyan Island today
Ma fee wagt kafy nerooh le jezerit bubyan elyoum

*This *isn't* a phrase book! The purpose of this book is *solely* to provide you with the tools to create *your own* sentences!

The Program

To happen – Yihsal
To order – Yitlob
To drink - Yishrab
Excuse me – Men fathlik/lo smaht **Child -** (**M**) Wild (**F**) Bint
Woman - Mara
To begin / to start – Yebda'
To finish – Yinhy/Ykalis
To help - Yisa'ed
To smoke - Yidakhin
To love - Yehib
To talk / to speak – Yitkallam

This must happen today
Hatha lazem yahsil el-youm
Excuse me, my child is here as well
Min fathlik, weldy hne baad
I love you
Ana ahebek
I see you
Ana ashoofak
I need you at my side
Ana ahtagik yamy
I need to begin soon to be able to finish at 3 o'clock in the afternoon
Ana ahtag abdy gariban ashan agder akalis elsa'a thlath el-asr
I need help
Ana ahtag mosa'ada
I don't want to smoke once again
Ana ma aby adakin marra thanya
I want to learn how to speak Arabic
Ana aby atalam shloon atkalam araby

Conversational Arabic Quick and Easy

To read - Yegra
To write - Yiktob
To teach - Yi'allim
To close - Yigfil
To choose - Yikhtar
To prefer - Yifathil
To put - Yihott
Less - Aggal
Sun - Shamss
Month – Shahr
I talk –Ysolf
Exact - Bithabt

I need this book to learn how to read and write in Arabic because I want to teach in Egypt
Ana ahtag hatha el-ketab ashan atalam shloon agra o akteb bel araby ashan aby adares eb maser
I want to close the door of the house
Ana aby asaker bab el-bait.
I prefer to put the gift here
Ana afathel ahett el-hadeya mne/hne
I want to pay less than you for the dinner
Ana aby adfaa aggal minnak hag el-asha
I speak with the boy and the girl in French
Ana atkalam ma elwalad o el-bent bil faransy
There is sun outside today
Fi shamss barra el-youm
Is it possible to know the exact date?
Momken ne'raf el-tawgeet bithabt?

*With the knowledge you've gained so far, now try to create your own sentences!

The Program

To exchange (money**)** – Taghyeer feloos
To call – Yedig
Brother – Akh
Dad – Obo
To sit - Yijlis
Together –Ma-bath
To change - Yetghayir
Of course - Tab'an / Akeed
Welcome - Ahlan wasahlan
During - Khelal
Years - Seneen
Sky - Sema
Up – Foog
Down - Taht
Sorry - Aseff
To follow - Yetba'
To the - Le
Big - Kbir
New - Jdid
Never / ever - Abadan

I don't want to exchange this money at the bank
Ana ma aby abadel elflus fe el-bank
I want to call my brother and my dad today
Ana aby adig 'ala okhoy w oboy el-youm
Of course I can come to the theater, and I want to sit together with you and with your sister
Tb'an hagdar aji lel msrah, w ana aby agad sawa wayak w waya okhtak
I need to go down to see your new house
Ana ahtag anzel tahat ashan ashoof baitik el-yedeed
I can see the sky from the window
Egdar ashoof el-sama min el-dreesha
I am sorry, but he wants to follow her to the store
Ana asef bas ohwa yaby ytbaha lama el-mahal
I don't ever want to see you again
Ana Ma aby ashofak marra thanya

*In Kuwaiti dialect, brother is *oko,* and dad is *obo*. However, "my dad" is *oboy* and "my brother" is *okhoy*. "My sister" is *ikhti*, and "my mother" is *omoy* *For the possessive pronouns, her (*ha*) and him (*a*), both become suffixes to the verb or noun. Concerning nouns: her house / *bait'ha,* his house / *bata*. Concerning cases regarding verbs, please see page 19.

To allow - Yismah
To believe – Yi'min
Morning – Sbaah
Except - Ila
To promise - Yiw'ed
Good night - Tisbah 'ala khair
To recognize - Yit'araf
People - Naas
To move - Yiharrik
Far - B'eed
Different - Mokhtalif
Man - Rayyal
To enter - Yidkhol
To receive – Yistilim
Throughout - Mn khilal
Good evening – Masa elkheir
Left / right - Ysar / Ymeen
Him / her – Ohwa / Ehya

I need to allow him to go with us, he is a different man now
Ana ahtag asmah la eye e mana. Ohuw rayal gaeer elheen.
I believe everything except this
ana bi'min b kol shay ila hatha
I promise to say good night to my parents each night
Ana wadit iny agool tesbah ala khaeer hag ahaly kill laila
The people from Kuwait are very pleasant
Elnass min elkuwait waied bashosheen
I need to find another hotel very quickly
Ana ahtag alga fendeg thany bsera'
They need to receive a book for work
Ohma yhtagon yestalmoon elketab hag elsogol
I see the sun in the morning
Ana ashoof el-shamss fel-sabaah
The house is on the right side of the street
El bait ala elganeb elyamen min elshare'

The Program

To wish - Yitmanna
Bad – Khayes/Mo-Zain
To get - Yakhith
To forget - Yinsa
Everybody / Everyone –Kel wahed / Elkel
Although - Ma' en
To feel - Yihis
Great – Ra'e'/Momtaz
Next (as in close, near) – Janb/Yam
Next (as in next year) - Jai
To like – Yehib
In front – Giddam
Person - Shakhs
Behind - Wara
Well –Zain
Restaurant – Mat'am
Bathroom – Dort elmoya / Twalet
Goodbye - Ma' elsalama

I don't want to wish you anything bad
Ana ma atmnalek ay shay mozain
I must forget everybody from my past to feel well
Ana lazem ansa kill elnas min el-mathy ashan aseer ahsan.
I am next to the person behind you
Ana yam elshaks ely warak
There is a great person in front of me
Fi shakhs mohm giddam
I say goodbye to my friends
Ana agol ma'a elslam hag rabee.
Where is the bathroom in the restaurant?
Wein elhamaam elly fel mt'aam?
She has to get a car before the next year
Heya me'taza tjeeb sayara gabl el-s'aani el jaia
I like the house, but it is very small
Ejabny el-bait, bass wayed sgeer.

*_Janb_ literally means "side." In Arabic, it refers to "next." _janby_ is "besides me" and _janbak_ is "besides you."

To remove / To take out - Yesheel
Please – Men fathlik/lo-samaht
Beautiful – Zayn / Helw
To lift – Yeshil / Yerfaa'
Include / Including - Yeshmal
Belong – Yintemy
To hold - Yimsik
To check – Yitfaggad
Small - Sgheer
Real - Hageegy
Week - Osboo'
Size - Gyaas
Even though – Ma' en
Doesn't - Mo
So (as in "then") – Ya'ny
So (as in "so big") –Wayed
Price – Thaman

She wants to remove this door please
Ehya taby tsheel hatha elbab lo samaht.
This doesn't belong here, I need to check again
Hatha mo hne, lazem ataked mara thanya.
This week the weather was very beautiful
Hatha el-esboo elgaw kan helo.
I need to know which is the real diamond
'Aani me'taz 'aref ayhom elmasa l-hageegyaa
Lazem a'aref elmasa el-segya.
We need to check the size of the house
Ehna lazem net'akad mn gyaas el bait
I want to lift this, so you need to hold it high
Aby arfa'a hatha, tehtag tshel hatha foog.
I can pay this even though that the price is expensive
Agdar adfa'a hatha, ma'a ena galy
Including everything is this price correct?
Yeshmal Kel shai, l-thaman saheh?

* Lo-samaht literally means it means "if you don't mind."

The Program

Countries of the Middle East
Dowal il-sharg il-awsat

Lebanon - Libnan
Syria - Surya
Jordan - Il-irdin
Saudi Arabia - Il-Suudiyah
Israel/Palestine/West Bank
Isra'il/Falastin/il-thiffih il-gharbiyyih
Bahrain - Il-Bahrain
Yemen - Yiman
Oman - 'Uman
United Arab Emirates - Il-Imarat
Kuwait - Il-Kuwait
Iraq - Il-'Iraq
Qatar - Gitar
Morocco - Il-Maghrib
Algeria - Il-yizayir
Libya - Libya
Egypt - Masir
Tunisia - Tunis

Months
January - Kanun il-thani
February - Shbat
March - Athar
April - Nisan
May - Ayyar
June - Huzayran
July - Tammuz
August - Aab
September - Aylul
October - Tishreen awwal
November - Tishreen thani
December - Kanun awwal

Days of the Week
Sunday - il-ahad
Monday - il-ithnin
Tuesday - il-thulatha'
Wednesday il-'arba'
Thursday - il-khamees
Friday - il-jim'a
Saturday – aissabt

Seasons
Spring - Rabee'
Summer - Saif
Autumn - Khareef
Winter – Ishta

Cardinal Directions
North Shimal
South Janoob
East Sharg
West Gharb

Colors
Black - (M)Aswad (F)Suda
White - (M)Abyath (F)Baitha
Gray - (M)Ramadi, (F)Ramadiyyih
Red - (M)Ahmar (F)Hamra
Blue - (M)Azrag (F)Zarga
Yellow - (M)Asfar (F)Safra
Green - (M)Akhthar (F)Khathra
Orange - (M)Burtuqali/(F)Burtuqaliyyih
Purple - (M) Banafsegy /(F) Banafsgia
Brown - (M) Bony(F) Bonyah

Numbers
One - Wahid
Two - Ithnain
Three - Thalathah
Four - Arba'
Five - Khams
Six - Sittah
Seven - Sab'
Eight - Tamanyih
Nine - Tis'
Ten - 'Ashr
Twenty - 'Ishreen
Thirty - Thalatheen
Forty - Arb'een
Fifty - Khamseen
Sixty - Sitteen
Seventy - Sab'een
Eighty - Thimaneen
Ninety - Tis'een
Hundred - Emyah
Thousand - Alf
Million – Milyun

Conversational Arabic Quick and Easy

BAHRAINI DIALECT

YATIR NITZANY

THE BAHRAINI DIALECT

The official language in Bahrain, similar to most Arabic-speaking countries, is Literary Arabic. This is a mixture of Classic Arabic and Modern Standard Arabic mixed with local dialects.

The local dialect is Bahrani Arabic (also known as Bahrani and Baharna Arabic, and called Baḥrāni by its speakers) and is a variety of Arabic spoken in Eastern Arabia and Oman. In Bahrain, the dialect is primarily spoken in Shia villages and some parts of Manama. It shares many features with Gulf Arabic dialects (e.g., those in Kuwait, UAE, Qatar) although it's not considered part of it by most linguists. General features include the Standard Arabic q becoming g (qamar vs gamar "moon") and J becoming y in some villages (jiḥḥe vs yiḥḥe "watermelon").

The total number of users of Bahrani in all countries is around 730,000.

The Bahrani Arabic dialect is meant to have been significantly influenced by the ancient Aramaic, Syriac, and Akkadian languages. It is one of three distinct dialects in Bahrain, with the other two being Sunni and Ajami Arabic. Sunni Bahrainis speak a dialect which is most similar to the urban dialect spoken in Qatar.

The Persian communities in Bahrain are commonly referred to as the Ajam and the Persian language is seen to have had the most foreign linguistic influence on all the Bahraini dialects. The differences between Bahrani Arabic and other Bahraini dialects suggest differing historical origins. The main differences between Bahrani and non-Bahrani dialects are evident in certain grammatical forms and pronunciation. Many Bahrani words have also been borrowed from Hindi, Turkish, or English

Spoken in: Bahrain

ARABIC PRONUNCIATIONS

PLEASE MASTER THE FOLLOWING PAGE IN ARABIC PRONUNCIATIONS PRIOR TO STARTING THE PROGRAM

Kha. For Middle Eastern languages including Arabic, Hebrew, Farsi, Pashto, Urdu, Hindi, etc., and also German, to properly pronounce the kh or ch is essential, for example, *Khaled* (a Muslim name) or *Chanukah* (a Jewish holiday) or *Nacht* ("night" in German). The best way to describe kh or ch is to say "ka" or "ha" while at the same time putting your tongue at the back of your throat and blowing air. It's pronounced similarly to the sound that you make when clearing your throat. Please remember this whenever you come across any word containing a kh in this program.

Ghayin. The Arabic gh is equivalent to the "g" in English, but its pronunciation more closely resembles the French "r," rather than "g." Pronounce it at the back of your throat. The sound is equivalent to what you would make when gargling water. Gha is pronounced more as "rha," rather than as "ga." *Ghada* is pronounced as "rhada." In this program, the symbol for *ghayin* is gh, so keep your eyes peeled.

Aayin is pronounced as a'a, pronounced deep at the back of your throat. Rather similar to the sound one would make when gagging. In the program, the symbol for *aayin* is a'a, u'u, o'o, or i'i.

Ha is pronounced as "ha." Pronunciation takes place deep at the back of your throat, and for correct pronunciation, one must constrict the back of the throat and exhale air while simultaneously saying "ha." In the program, this strong h ("ha") is emphasized whenever *ha, ah, hi, he,* or *hu* is encountered.

NOTE TO THE READER

The purpose of this book is merely to enable you to communicate in the Bahraini Arabic dialect. In the program itself (pages 17-38) you may notice that the composition of some of those sentences might sound rather clumsy. This is intentional. These sentences were formulated in a specific way to serve two purposes: to facilitate the easy memorization of the vocabulary and to teach you how to combine the words in order to form your own sentences for quick and easy communication, rather than making complete literal sense in the English language. So keep in mind that this is not a phrase book!

As the title suggests, the sole purpose of this program is for conversational use only. It is based on the mirror translation technique. These sentences, as well as the translations are not incorrect, just a little clumsy. Latin languages, Semitic languages, and Anglo-Germanic languages, as well as a few others, are compatible with the mirror translation technique.

Many users say that this method surpasses any other known language learning technique that is currently out there on the market. Just stick with the program and you will achieve wonders!

Note to the Reader

Again, I wish to stress this program is by no means, shape, or form a phrase book! The sole purpose of this book is to give you a fundamental platform to enable you to connect certain words to become conversational. Please also read the "Introduction" and the "About Me" section prior to commencing the program.

In order to succeed with my method, please start on the very first page of the program and fully master one page at a time prior to proceeding to the next. Otherwise, you will overwhelm yourself and fail. Please do not skip pages, nor start from the middle of the book.

It is a myth that certain people are born with the talent to learn a language, and this book disproves that myth. With this method, anyone can learn a foreign language as long as he or she follows these explicit directions:

* Memorize the vocabulary on each page

* Follow that memorization by using a notecard to cover the words you have just memorized and test yourself.

* Then read the sentences following that are created from the vocabulary bank that you just mastered.

* Once fully memorized, give yourself the green light to proceed to the next page.

Again, if you proceed to the following page without mastering the previous, you are guaranteed to gain nothing from this book. If you follow the prescribed steps, you will realize just how effective and simplistic this method is.

The Program

Let's Begin! "Vocabulary" (Memorize the Vocabulary)

I | I am - Ana
With you – **(M)** Ma'ak / weyak / **(F)** Ma'ach / weyach
With him / With her – **(M)** Ma'ah / weyah/ **(F)** Ma'aaha/ weyaha
With us - Ma'ana / weyanh
For you - (M) Lek (F) lech.
Without him – Bedonah
Without them – (M and F) Bedonhom
Always – Dayman / doum
Was - Kan
This, This is – Hay
Is, it's, it is – Hay
Sometimes – Ahyanan / Sa'aat
Maybe – Momken / Yumken
You / You are / Are you - (M)Enta? / (F)Enti?
You (plural) – Entow / enton
Is it? – (M) Ohwa / (F) Ehya
Today - Elyoum
Better - Ahsan, afdhal
With them - Weyahom / Ma'aahom
For them - Hag'hom / Lhum
He / He is – Ohwa
She / She is – Ehya
From / From where - Min / Min wein

This is for you
(M) Hay lek / (F) Hay lech
I am from Bahrain
Ana min el Bahrain
Are you from Manama?
(M)Enta min manama / (F) Inti min Manama
I am with you
(M)Ana ma'ak / ana weyak
(F)Ana ma'ach / ana weyach
Sometimes you are with us at the mall
Ahyanan/sa'aat enta maa'ana fe el mojama'
I am always with her
Ana dayman ma'aha
Are you without them today?
(m)Enta bedonhom el yom /(f) enti bedonhom el yom
Sometimes I am with him
Ahyanan bkoun ma'ah / weyah

*In Bahraini Arabic, there are gender rules. Saying "for you" to a male is *lek*, but if you are talking to a female, it's *lech*.

I was - Ana kent
To be - (M)Ykun / (F) Tkun
The – Al
Same – Nafasah / methleh
Good – Zain \ Tamam
Here – Ehni
Very – Wayed
And - Wa
Between - Beyn
Now – Tawa / Aheen
Later / After / afterwards – Ba'adeen
If – Law / itha
Yes – Ee / na'am
To – *(going to)* ila, il
Tomorrow – Bacher
You – **(M)** Enta / (F) Enti
Also / too / as well – Hata / Ba'ad

If it's between now and later
Law kan bain aheen w ba'adeen
It's better tomorrow
Bacher Ahsan
This is good as well
Hay ba'ad zain
To be the same person
'Ashan eykon nafs elshakhs
Yes, you are very good
Ee, enta wayed zain
I was here with them
Ana kent ma'ahom hni / ana kent hni ma'ahom
You and I
(M) ana w enta / (F) ana w enti
The same day
Nafs elyoum

Me – (read footnote)
Ok – Tamam/ inzain / ok
Even if - Hatta itha / hatta law
No – La'
Worse - Aswa' / akhas
Where - Waen
Everything – Kelshay
Somewhere – Fe mukan mo'ayen
What – Shenow
Almost – Taqreeban
There – Ehnaak

Afterwards is worse
Ba'deen akhas/aswa'
Even if I go now
Hatta law reht aheen
Where is everything?
Weyn kel shi?
Maybe somewhere
Yamken fe mukan mo'yen
What? I am almost there
Shenow? Ana taqreban wessalt
Where are you?
(M)Weynak?- (F) Weynach
Where is the airport?
Wein el-matar?
Where is the embassy?
Wein al sifara?

*In Bahraini dialect, there are a few ways of expressing negations; *laa, mabi, mo.* Depending on where it falls in the sentence. For verbs we use *mabi*, "I don't want" /*ana mabi*. Regarding adjectives we use *mo*, "I am not here" / *ana mo hne*. But to simply say "no" we use *laa*, for example if asked something like, "are you going?" you would answer, *laa*, to indicate "no."

Nouns ending in a vowel end with –ti. Nouns ending with a consonant end with –y.
For example; cousin / Eyaal 'Ami, my cousin / for the male cousin: *Weld 'Ami* and *Bent 'Ami* for the female cousin or "cup" / *koub*, "my cup" / *koubi*
- For second

*In Arabic, the pronoun "me" has several definitions. In relation to verbs, it's *le*. *Le* refers to any verb that relates to the action of doing something to someone or for someonee

For example, "tell me," "tell (to) me" / (M) *qool le*.
'alay just means "me": "love me" / *hebni*
Other variations (*ya*):
  * "on me" / *'aley*, "in me" /*fini*
  * "to me" / *'hagi*, "with me" / *ma'ay - weyay*

The same rule applies for "him" and "her"—both become suffixes: *–I* and *–a*. Basically all verbs pertinent to male end with *h*, and all pertinent to female end with *ha*.
  * "love her" / *hebha*, "love him" / *hebih*
  * "love them" /(M) *hebhom* / (F) *Hebihom*, "love us" / *hebna*

Any verb that relates to doing someone to someone, for someone put *l*:
  * "tell her" / *qool-lha*, "tell him" / *qool-loh*
  * "tell them" / *qool-lehom*, "tell us" / *qool-lena*

Adding you as a suffix in Arabic is *ek*, female *ech*
  * "love you" /(M) *ahbek* / (F) *ahbech*, "tell you" / (M) *qool-ek*/ (F) *qool-ech*

House – Beit
In, at, at the – Fi el/il/Al
Car – Sayyarah
Already - Asasan
Good morning - Sabah el-kheyr
How are you? - (M) Shlounek (F) shlounech
Where are you from? - (M) Min weyn enta? (F) Min weyn Inti?
Hello – Hala
What is your name? - (M) Shenow esmak / (F) shenow esmech
How old are you? - (M) Cham Umrik (F) Cham Umrich
Son – Weld
Daughter – Bent
I have – Ana 'endi
Doesn't *or* **isn't –** Mabi / mo / ma (see footnotes on previous page)
Hard - Sa'ab
Still – Lilhin
Then (or "so") – Ma'naha / yaa'ni

She doesn't have a car, so maybe she is still at the house
Ehya ma'endeha Seyyarah, fa ya'ni ahya lilhin fe elbet
I am in the car already with your son and daughter
Ana fe elsayyarah ma' bintek w wildik
Good morning, how are you today?
Sabah elkheir, (M)shoulnik/(F)shlounech elyoum
Hello, what is your name?
Halla, shenow esmek(M)/esmech(F)
How old are you?
(M) Cham umrik, (F) cham umrich
This is very hard, but it's not impossible
Hay wayed sa'eb bas mo mostahil
Where are you from?
Min weyn (M) enta / (F) inti?

*In Bahraini, possessive pronouns become suffixes to the noun. For example, for the English word "your," *ek or ik* is the masculine form, and *ech or ich* feminine form.
- "your book" / *kitabek* (m.), *kitabich* (f.), "your house" / *betek* (m.), *betch*(f.)
While speaking to a female the noun ending countains a "ch":
"Your sisters" – *khawatich*, "Your car" - *sayyartich* , "Your house" - *beitch*
While speaking to a male the noun ending contains a "k":
"Your sisters" – *khawatik*, "Your car" - *sayyartik* , "Your house" - *beitik*
*In Arabic, as well as in other Semitic languages, the article "a" doesn't exist. "She doesn't have a car" / *Ahya ma'endeha sayyarah.*
**"So" could also mean *ya'ni* if we mean "so that means."

Thank you – shokran
For – 'Ashan / hag
Anything – Ay shay
That, That is – (M) Thaak – (F) Theech
Time – Wagt *(see footnote)*
But – Laken / Bas
No – La'
I am not – Ana mo
Away - B'eed
Late - Meta'akhir
Similar – Nafs
Another/ other – Gheir / shay thani
Side – Tarref
Until – Lin
Yesterday – Ams
Without us – Bedunna/Mn gherna
Since – Min lamma
Day - Yom
Before – Gabel

Thanks for everyything
Shukran 'ala kelshay
It's almost time
Saar alwgt taqreebn
I am not here, I am away
Ana mo hni, ana ba'eed
That is a similar house
Hay nfs albeit
I am from the other side
Ana min aljeha althania
But I was here until late yesterday
Bas ana kent hni ams len wagt mota'kher
I am not at the other house
Ana mo fil elbeit althani

---

*In Bahraini Arabic, there are three definitions for time:
* "time" / *waqt* refers to "era", "moment period," "duration of time."
* "time(s)" / *Sa'aa(t)* / Awga*(t)* refers to "occasion" or "frequency."
* "time" / *sa'a* references "hour," "what time is it?"
This isn't a phrase book! The purpose of this book is solely to provide you with the tools to create your own sentences!

What time is it? – El sa'a cham?
I say / I am saying - Ana agool / ana ga'ed agool
I want – Aby
Without you – (M) bedounik – (F) bedounech
Everywhere /wherever – Fe kel mokan/ ay mokan
I go to – (M) ana rayeh – (F) ana rayeha
With - Ma'a
My – Li / mali
Cousin (paternal) - (M)Wild 'ami (P) "Eyaal 'Ami" (F)Bent "Ami" (P)Banat "Ami",
Cousin (Maternal) – (M) Wild khali /(P) "Eyaal Khali" /(P) Bent khali
I need - Ana mohtaj/ahtaj /lazim (in this program will be used interchangeably)
Right now – Tawa / Haleyan
Night – Fleyl
To see – Ashan tchouf (M) – Ashan tchoufin (F)
Light – Dhau / leyt / nour
Outside - Barra
Without - Bidoun / minghir
Happy – Mestanis (M) – Mestansa(F)
I see / I am seeing – Achouf / Ana ga'ed achouf

I am saying no / I say no
Ana agoul la / ana gelt la
I want to see this today
Aabi achouf hay alyoum
I am with you everywhere
Ana ma'ak fi kel mokan
I am happy without my cousins here
(M)Ana mestans bedon eyaal 'ami hni (F) ana mestansa bedon eyaal 'ami hni.
I need to be there at night
Lazim akoun hnak fleyl
I see light outside
Achouf nour/leyt bara'
What time is it right now?
El sa'a cham aheen?

---

*"Mine" - *li/I* is also a possessive pronoun. *li* means "my" but also becomes a suffix to a noun.
"cousin" / *weld al'am*, "my cousin" /weld 'ami,"cup" / *koob*, "my cup" / *koobi*
For second and third person masculine noun, *weld* ("son"), male (S) *ik*, (P) *kom*) and female (S) *ich*, (P) *kom*). "His" –*'eh'/* "hers" – *ha*, noun endings will be *eh* (for male) and *ha* (for female).
"your son" / *Wildik* (m.), *Wildich* (f.), "your (plural) son" / *Wildkom* (m.) (f.), "his son" / *Wild'h*, "her son" / *Wildha*, "our son" / *Waladna* , "their son" / *Wildhom (m.)*, *Wildhom(f.)*
For second and third person feminine noun: "car" / *sayyara*.
"your car" / *Sayyartak(m) sayyartech (f)*, "your (plural) car" / *Sayyartkom*, "his car" / *Sayyart'h*, "her car" / *Sayyart'ha*, "our car" / *Sayyartna*, "their car" / *Sayyart'hom*

Place – Mukan
Easy - Sahel
To find – 'Ashan et lagi / Ashan et'hasel
To look for/to search – 'Edawwer
Near / Close – Jreeb
To wait – Yantter
To sell – Etbee'
To use – Yesta'amil
To know – Ya'ref
To decide – Ashan yeqarir
Between - Beyn
Both – Ethneenhom
Next to – Yam

This place is easy to find
Hay almokan sahel t'hasleh
I want to look for this next to the car
Abi adawwer hay yam alsayyara
I am saying to wait until tomorrow
Ana agoul nanter len bacher
This table is easy to sell (to be sold)
Hay eltawla sahel tenba'
I want to use this
Nabi nesta'mel hay
I need to know where is the house
Abi a'arf wen albeit
I want to decide between both places
Abi Akhtar bein almokaneen
I need to find the hospital
Lazim a'arf wein almostashfa

*In Bahraini Arabic, "to sell" is (M) *Etbee'* / (F) *Etbee'in* For "to be sold", we use *Tenbaa'* or feminine and *'Yenbaa'* for masculine.

Because - 'Ashan /le'anna
To buy – 'Ashan teshtree
They – Ohma
Them, their – Ohma
Bottle – Gharsha
Beach - Bahar
Book - Ktab
Mine – Li / mali
To understand – 'Ashan nafham/ tefham
Problem / Problems - (S) Moshkla / (P) Mashahkill
I do / I am doing - Ana aswe / ana ga'ed aswe
Of - Min
To look – Etchouf
Myself - Brohe
Enough - Khalas / ekfaya
Food / water - Akill / Maay
Each/ every/ entire/ all – Kel / ay / kilah
Hotel – Fondoq

I like this hotel because I want to look at the beach
Ajbni alfondoq la'anh abi atalea' albahar
I want to buy a bottle of water
Abi ashtrey gharshat may
I do this every day
Aswe hay kel youm
Both of them have enough food
Athneenhom 'end'hom akel kefayyah
That is the book, and that book is mine
Hay ohwa alktab, w hathak alktab mali
I need to understand the problem
Ahtaj afham almoshkla
I see the view of the city from the hotel
Achouf almadina mn alfondoq
I do my homework today
Aswe wajby alyoum
My entire life (*all my life*)
Toul hayati\ kil hayati \ omri kilah

*There are two ways of saying "life" in Bahraini: *'omr* and *hayaaty*.

I like – Ya'jbni
There Is / There are – Fe
There – Hnak
Family / Parents - Al ahal / omi w uboi / alwalid w alwalidah
Why – Lesh
To say – Engool
Something – Shay
To go – Namshy
Ready – Jahiz / bariz
Soon – Jreeb
To work – 'Ashan neshtghl
Who – Meno / Min
To know - 'Ashan naarif
That (conjunction) – Edha / inna

I like to be at my house with my parents
Aheb akoun fe beyti ma' uboi w umi
I want to know why I need to say something important
Abi a'ref lesh lazim agoul shay mohm
I am there with him
Ana ehnak weyah/ma'ah
I am busy, but I need to be ready soon
Ana mashghool, bas lazm abriz ebser'aa
I like to go to work
Ahb arouh aldawam/ alshghul
'Who is there?
Min hnak
I want to know if they are here, because I want to go outside
Abi a'ref edha ohma ehnak, la'na abi attla'
There are seven dolls
Fe saba' lei'aab
I need to know that it is a good idea
Abi a'ref edha hay fekra zaina

*In the last sentence, we use "that" as a conjunction (*edha*) and as a demonstrative pronoun *haady*.

How much /How many – Cham / shkether?
To bring – Enyeeb
With me - M'aay
Instead - Bedal
Only - Bas
When – Meta
Or – Walah
I can / Can I - Ana agdar / agdar ana?
Were - Kan
Without me - Bedouni
Fast - Ebser'a
Slow – Batee' / bil'adal
Cold – Brd
Inside - Dakhel
To eat – Bnakel
Hot – Harr
To Drive – Bensoog

How much money do I need to bring with me?
Cham lazim ayeeb ma'aay
Instead of this cake, I want that cake
Bedal thy alcake aby hathak alcake
Only when you can
Bas lamma tagder.
They were without me yesterday
Ohma ams kanow bedouni
Do I need to drive the car fast or slow?
Lazim asoug alsayyarah besr'a wla bilaa'dal
It is cold inside the library
Bard dakhel almaktba?
Yes, I like to eat this hot for my lunch
Ee aheb alakl alhaar hag alghadaa
I can work today
Agdar ashteghl alyoum

*"Were" is *kano*, but for "they were,". "We were" is *kenna*
*"I can" and "can I?" could either be *ana agder* "You can" or "can you?" *is enta tagdir?*

To answer – Enjaweb
To fly – Benteer /Enteer
Time / Times - Waget / Awgaat
To travel – Ensafer
To learn – Netaalem
How – Shloun
To swim – Nesbah
To practice – 'Ashan netmarin
To play - Nal'ab
To leave - Namshi
Many /much /a lot – Wayed
I go to – Enrouh
First - Al awal
Time / Times – Marra/Marrat, sa'a / sa'aat (footnote)

I want to answer many questions
Abi ajaweb wayed as'ela
I must fly to Dubai today
Lazim ateer le dubai alyoum
I need to learn how to swim at the pool
Lazim at'alam atsbah fil brcha
I want to learn to play better tennis
Abi at'alm al'ab tennis ahsan.
I want to leave this here for you when I go to travel the world
Abi akhli hay hni hagek lin basafer al'alam
Since the first time
Men awal marra
The children are yours
Al 'eyaal lik

*In Bahraini, "to leave (something)" is *eykhaly*. "To leave (a place)" is *yemshee*.

*In Bahraini Arabic, there are three definitions for time:
- "time" / *waqt* refers to "era", "moment period," "duration of time."
- "time(s)" / *Sa'aa(t)* / Awga*(t)* refers to "occasion" or "frequency."
- "time" / *sa'a* references "hour," "what time is it?"

*With the knowledge you've gained so far, now try to create your own sentences!

Nobody / anyone – Ma fee had/ Ay had
Against – Dhed
Us – Ehna
To visit - Enzoor
Mom / Mother - Yomma / Omy
To give – Naa'ty
Which – 'Aay
To meet - Netlaga
Someone – Wahed
Just - Bas
To walk – Netmasha
Around – Yam, dar ma daar
Towards - Jehet
Than - Min
Nothing – Mafeshy / wla shay

Something is better than nothing
Shay ahsan min wala shay
I am against him
Ana dheda ohwa
Is there anyone here?
Fi ahad ehni
We go to visit my family each week
Ehna enzour ahlna kil asbou'
I need to give you something
Lazim a'teek shay
Do you want to go meet someone?
Tabi trouh tchous wahed?
I was here on Wednesdays as well
Ana kent hni youm alarba'aa ba'ad
Do you do this every day?
Tswe hay kil youm?
You need to walk around, but not towards the house
Enta lazim tamshi dar ma dar albet bas mo jehat albet

---

*In Bahraini, when using the pronoun "you" as a direct and indirect object pronoun (the person who is actually affected by the action that is being carried out) in relation to a verb, the pronoun "you" becomes a suffix to that verb. That suffix becomes *ak* (masc.) *ik* (fem.).

- "to give" / *ta'teeh*:
- "to give you" / *'ashan a'teek*
- "to tell" / *agoul*
- "to tell you" / *agoul-lik* (m.), *agoul-lich* (f.)
- "see you" / *achoufik*:
- "to see you" (plural) / *achoufkom*

I have – 'Endy
Don't – Mo, Mabi
Friend – Rfeejy / sadeeqy
To borrow – Netsalef
To look like / resemble – Yeshbah
Like (preposition) - Methl / nafs
Grandfather – Yaddy
To want – Naby
To stay – Tag'ed
To continue – Etkamil
Way – Tareej
I don't - Maby
To show – Enrawwy
To prepare – Enjahiz / enbariz
I am not going - Ana mo rayeh

Do you want to look like Salim
Tebe teshbah salim?
I want to borrow this book for my grandfather
Abi ast'eer alktab hag yaddy
I want to drive and to continue on this way to my house
Aby asoug w akmel 'ala hay altreej hag beity
I have a friend there, that's why I want to stay in Manama
Endy rfeej ehnak, ashan chithi abi atim f almanama
I am not going to see anyone here
Ana mabchouf ay ahad hni
I need to show you how to prepare breakfast
Lazm araweek shloun tswe reyoug
Why don't you have the book?
Lesh ma'endak alktab?
That is incorrect, I don't need the car today
Hay mabi sah, ana mo mahtaj alsayyara alyom

To remember – 'Ashan tit'thaker
Your – Leek / malik
Number - Ragm
Hour - Sa'aa
Dark / darkness - thalam – Emathlem
About / on the - Ala = 'Ann
Grandmother – Yaddah
Five - Khamsa
Minute / minutes - Dgeega/ dgayg
More – Akthar
To think – 'Aashan etfakir
To do – Ensawi
To come – Enyey
To hear - Nasma'
Last – Akher

You need to remember my number
Lazim tt'thaker raqmi
This is the last hour of darkness
Hay akher sa'aat thalam
I want to come and to hear my grandmother speak Arabic
Aby ayey 'ashan asma' yadti tetkalam 'araby
I need to think more about this, and what to do
Ahtaj afker akthr fe thy w fe sheno baswe
From here to there, it's only five minutes
Min hni li hnak, bas khams degayeg
The school on the mountain
El madresa fog aljabal

To leave – Emshy
Again - Ba'ad marra
Bahrain - Bahrain
To take - Akhed
To try – Etjareeb
To rent – 'Ajer
Without her – Bdonnha
We are – Ehna
To turn off – 'Sik
To ask – Tas'el
To stop – Enwagef
Permission – Edhen/ este'than

He needs to leave and rent a house at the beach
Ohwa lazm yetla' w ye'ajer beit 'ala albahar
I want to take the test without her
Aby aswe alemtehan bedounha
We are here a long time
Ehna hni mn zman
I need to turn off the lights early tonight
Ahtaj a'sik al leytat min wgt al-leyla
We want to stop here
Nabi nuwgaf ehni
We are from Zallaq
Ehna min al zallaq
The same building
Nafs el mabna
I want to ask permission to leave
Abi ast'thin 'ashan amshy

*In Bahraini, "to stop" is *nwagef* but "to cease" is *khalas*. For example, if someone is bothering you, you tell them, "Stop!" / *Khalas!*
*In Bahraini, when one is speaking of themselves an "a" or "ba" is added as a prefix preceding verb. For example, "to rent" - *ajer* but "I will rent" ba'ajer.

To open – Naftah
A bit, a little, a little bit – Eshwaya(F) / eshwy(M)
To pay – Tadfa'
Once again - Marra thanya / ba'ad/ ba'ad mara
There isn't/ there aren't - Mafy
Sister – Ekht
To hope – Nitmana
To live - 'Ashan n'eesh
Nice to meet you – (M)Tesharrafna bma'rftak, (F)tesharrafna bma'riftich
Name - Ism
Last name - Al laqab
To return – Terj'a
Manama – El manama
Door – Bab

I need to open the door for my sister
Lazim abattel al bab hag ekthi
I need to buy something
Mohtaj ashtry shay
I want to see your sisters
Abi achouf khawatik (M) / abi achouf khawatich (F)
Nice to meet you, what is your name and your last name
Teshrft bm'ariftik, shenow esmk w laqabik? (Footnote)
To hope for a little better
Bnetmanna a'san ahsan shwaya
I want to return from the United States and to live in Qatar without problems
Ane nebe nerja' mn amerika w n'eesh fe Qatar bala mashkal
Why are you sad right now?
'Alash ente hazeen tawa?
There aren't any people here
Mafeesh naas hena
There isn't enough time to go to Al Muharraq today
Mafeesh wagit ey sid 'ala khatir nimsho le al muharraq elyoum

*In Bahraini, regarding the verb "to meet" there are two separate cases to define this verb; *tejtehme'* and *abil*. Depending of the context: to meet for business is *tejtehme'* like in the sentence "do you want to go meet someone?" However, for meeting the sister, is getting acquainted with her, here it's *'abill*.
This *isn't* a phrase book! The purpose of this book is *solely* to provide you with the tools to create *your own* sentences!

To happen – Eyseer
To order – Ettleb
To drink - Teshrab
Excuse me - Law semaht(M) – law semahti (F).
Child - Yahel
Woman - Marrah
To begin / to start - Nebtedi
To finish – Yekhaliss
To help - Eysa'ed
To smoke – Edakhin
To love –Et'heb
To talk / to speak – Titkalim

This must happen today
Hay lazim yessier el youm
Excuse me, my child is here as well
Law semaht, hatta weldi hni
I love you
(M) Ana ahebik, (F) ana ahebich
I see you
(M) Achoufik/ achoufich(F)
I need you at my side
Ana mohtaj lik yami
I need to begin soon to be able to finish at 'o'clock in the afternoon
Lazim abtedi ebser'a ashan akhaliss al aser
I need help
Ana mohtaj mosaa'da
I don't want to smoke once again
Ana mabi adakhen ba'ad marra.
I want to learn how to speak Arabic
Abi at'alam atklam 'araby

*"To help" is *sa'ed*. However, "help!" is *mosa'adah*. "I need help" or "I need rescue" / *ana moh'taj musa'da*
*"To be able to" is *'ashan akoun gader'*

To read – Tegra
To write – Tekteb
To teach - Et'aalem
To close – Etssik
To choose – Tekhtaar
To prefer - Etfadil
To put - Et'hett
Less – Aqal
Sun - Shames
Month - Shaher
I talk - Ana atkalam
Exact – Bildhabat

I need this book to learn how to read and write in Arabic because I want to teach in Egypt
Ahtaj hay alktab ashan at'alam agra wo aktib 'araby la'na abi adares fe masser
I want to close the door of the house
Abi assik bab albeit
I prefer to put the gift here
Afdhel ahett alhadeya hni
I want to pay less than you for the dinner
Abi adafa' aqel mink hag al 'asha
I speak with the boy and the girl in French
Ana aklim albint w alwalad faransi
There is sun outside today
Fi shamess baraa elyoum
Is it possible to know the exact date?
Yessier a'ref altareekh bildhabit

To exchange (money**)** – Nassref
To call – Netissel
Brother – Ukhoy
Dad – Uboi/ al walid/ baba
To sit - Nag'ed
Together - Ma'a ba'adh
To change – Nekhtar
Of course - Akeed
During - Mabaen
Years - **(S)**Seneh / **(P)** Esneen
Sky – Elsamaa
Up – Foog
Down – Tahat
Sorry – Asef (m) – asefa(f)
To follow - Tabie'
To the – El
Big – 'Ouad
New – Yedeed
Never / ever – Abadan / abad

I don't want to exchange this money at the bank
Ana mabi assref alflous fe el bank
I want to call my brother and my dad today
Ana abi atessel fe ukhoi w uboi alyoum
Of course I can come to the theater, and I want to sit together with you and with your sister
Aked agdar ayey almasrah, w abi aga'ed ma'ak w ma'a ekhtik.
I need to go down to see your new house
Lazm anzil tahat 'ashan achouf beitk alyedeed
I can see the sky from the window
Agdar achouf el sama min aldareesha.
I am sorry, but he wants to follow her to the store
Ana assef bas ohwa yabi yerouh al mahal
I don't want to see you again
Ana mabi achoufk ba'ad

*In Bahraini dialect, brother is *okhow,* and dad is *ubow,* However, "my dad" is *ubooy* and "my brother" is *okhooy.* "My sister" is *ekhti,* and "my mother" is *ommy*

*For the possessive pronouns, him (*h*) and her (h*a*), both become suffixes to the verb or noun. Concerning nouns: her house / *beit'ha,* his house / *beit'h.* Concerning cases regarding verbs.

To allow – Yesmah / yekhali
To believe – Etsadeg
Morning – Sobah
Except - Ela
To promise - Toow'ed
Good night - Tesbah 'ala kheir
To recognize – At'araf
People – Naas
Welcome – Ahlan/ afwan (footnote)
To move – Et'harek
Far - Eb'eed
Different – Gher
Man – Rayyal
To enter – Etdesh
To receive – Testalem
Throughout - Ma been
Good evening – Masaa el kheir
Left / right - Yessar/ yemeen
Him / her - Ohwa / ahya

I need to allow him to go with us, he is a different man now
Abik etkhalih yerouh maa'ana, ohwa rayyal hani aheen.
I believe everything except this
Asadeg kelshay ela hay.
I promise to say good night to my parents each night
Waa'ad amase ala umi w uboi kel youm
The people from Jordan are very pleasant
Elnas ele min al ordon wayed ehleywin
I need to find another hotel very quickly
Lazim ahasel fondoq thani ebser'aa
They need to receive a book for work
Lazm yestalmon ketab hag alshoghul.
I see the sun in the morning
Ana achouf alshams alssobah
The house is on the right side of the street
El beit ele 'ala yemeen alshare'

*In Bahraini dialect, the use of "welcome" as a greeting would be *ahlan/ ahleen/ hala*. However, the use of "welcome" as a reply to "thank you" would be *afwan*.

*With the knowledge you've gained so far, now try to create your own sentences!

To wish - Netmana
Bad – Mob zain
To get – Et-hasal
To forget - Tansa
Everybody / Everyone - Kel alnas/ kelhom/ kelman
Although - Maa' inna
To feel – 'Ashan et-hes
Great – Wayed zain
Next (as in close, near) - Yam / jereeb
Next (as in next year) - El yayh
To like – Ya'jebni
In front – Jedam
Person – Shakhs
Behind – Wara
Well – Anzain
Restaurant - Mat'em
Bathroom – Hammam
Goodbye – Ma'a alsalaama

I don't want to wish you anything bad
Ana mabi atemna lik shay mo zain
I must forget everybody from my past to feel well
Ana lazim ansa alkil min madheyye 'ashan aseer ahsan.
I am next to the person behind you
Ana yam alshakhs ele warak
There is a great person in front of me
Fe shakhs wayed zain jedamy
I say goodbye to my friends
Ana agool ma'a alsalama hag rab'ee.
Where is the bathroom in the restaurant?
Ween el hamaam ili felmat'em?
She has to get a car before the next year
Ahya lazim teshtery sayyara gabel al senna alyayah
I like the house, but it is very small
'Ajabni albeit, bas wayed esgheer

To remove / to take out – Sheelh/ wadeh bara'
Please - Law samaht / 'aaad.
Beautiful - Helo
To lift – 'Shan tarfaa'
Include / Including – Shamel / Yeshmal
Belong – Melk
To hold – Eyawed
To check – Net'akad
Small - Esgheer
Real - Sij
Week - Esboo'
Size – Mqas / hajim / size
Even though - Hatta law
So (as in "then") – Anzain / ya'ni
So (as in "so big") - Wayed
Price - Se'er

She wants to remove this door please
Ehya tabi etsheel hay albab law semaht
This doesn't belong here, I need to check again
Hay mukaneh mo ehni, lazim achayek mara thania
This week the weather was very beautiful
Hal asbou' aljaw wayed helo
I need to know which is the real diamond
Abi a'aref ay wahed ohwa al almas alsejji
We need to check the size of the house
Lazim enchayek hajim albeit
I want to lift this, so you need to hold it high
Abi asheel hay f enta lazim etyawdeh foug
I can pay this even though that the price is expensive
Agdar adfa' se'r hay hatta w ahwa ghali
Including everything is this price correct?
Alse'r yeshmal kelshy sah?

Other useful tools in Bahraini

Countries of the Middle East
Buldan alsharq al-awsatt

Lebanon - Lebnan
Syria - Suriyya
Jordan -ordon
Saudi Arabia - Els'oodya
Israel /Palestine /West Bank - Isra'eel / Falsteen / eldaffa el-Gharbeyyeh
Bahrain - L-Bahrain
Yemen - L-Yamen
Oman - 'Oman
United Arab Emirates - L-Emarat
Kuwait - L-Kweit
Iraq - L-'Iraq
Qatar – Gettar
Morocco - L-Maghreb
Algeria - L-Jaza'ir
Libya - Leebya
Egypt - Maser
Tunisia – Tonis

Months

January - Ynayr
February - Febrayr
March – Mares
April - Ebreel
May - May
June - Yunyu
July – Yulyu
August – Aghustus
September – Sebtamber
October - Oktobar
November – Novamber
December – Dicembar

Days of the Week

Sunday – El ahed
Monday - El athneen
Tuesday – Thulatha'/el thaltha
Wednesday - El arbe'aa
Thursday - Elkhamees
Friday - El jom'aa
Saturday - El sabet

Seasons

Spring – El rebee'
Summer - Elseef
Autumn - Elkhareef
Winter – El shetta'

Cardinal Directions

North - Shamaal
South - Jonoob
East – El Sharq'
West – El ghareb

Conversational Arabic Quick and Easy

OMANI ARABIC

YATIR NITZANY

OMANI ARABIC DIALECT

The current population of the Sultanate of Oman is estimated to be 4,720,483. The country is on the southeastern coast of the Arabian Peninsula. Oman is at the mouth of the Persian Gulf and shares land borders with the United Arab Emirates to the northwest, Saudi Arabia to the west, and Yemen to the southwest. It shares marine borders with Iran and Pakistan. The coast is formed by the Arabian Sea on the southeast and the Gulf of Oman on the northeast.

The official language is Arabic, but prior to Islam, central Oman lay outside of the core area of spoken Arabic. The Mehri language used to be widespread in the areas around alālah in afār and westward into the Yemen, and until the 18th or 19th century it was spoken further north.

Besides Arabic, the main languages spoken in Oman are English, Baluchi (Southern Baluchi), Urdu, and various Indian languages. English is taught at school from an early age, is widely spoken in the business community, a\d almost all signs and writings appear in both Arabic and English at tourist sites. Baluchi is the mother tongue of the Baloch people from Balochistan in western Pakistan, eastern Iran, and southern Afghanistan, and is widely spoken in Oman. A significant number of residents also speak Urdu due to Pakistani migration in the late 1980s and 1990s and additionally, due to historical relations with Zanzibar, Swahili is also widely spoken.

Endangered indigenous languages in Oman include Kumzari, Bathari, Harsusi, Hobyot, Jibbali, and Mehri. At the most basic level, there are two kinds of dialects, those of settlers and those of Bedouin who reached eastern and south-eastern Arabia up to the 18th century, and they share some features. Omani dialects preserve much vocabulary that has been lost in other Arabic dialects.

Spoken in: Oman

ARABIC PRONUNCIATIONS

PLEASE MASTER THE FOLLOWING PAGE IN ARABIC PRONUNCIATIONS PRIOR TO STARTING THE PROGRAM

Kha. For Middle Eastern languages including Arabic, Hebrew, Farsi, Pashto, Urdu, Hindi, etc., and also German, to properly pronounce the kh or ch is essential, for example, *Khaled* (a Muslim name) or *Chanukah* (a Jewish holiday) or *Nacht* ("night" in German). The best way to describe kh or ch is to say "ka" or "ha" while at the same time putting your tongue at the back of your throat and blowing air. It's pronounced similarly to the sound that you make when clearing your throat. Please remember this whenever you come across any word containing a kh in this program.

Ghayin. The Arabic *gh* is equivalent to the "g" in English, but its pronunciation more closely resembles the French "r," rather than "g." Pronounce it at the back of your throat. The sound is equivalent to what you would make when gargling water. Gha is pronounced more as "rha," rather than as "ga." *Ghada* is pronounced as "rhada." In this program, the symbol for ghayin is gh, so keep your eyes peeled.

Aayin is pronounced as *a'a,* pronounced deep at the back of your throat. Rather similar to the sound one would make when gagging. In the program, the symbol for *aayin* is *a'a, u'u, o'o,* or *i'i.*

Ha is pronounced as "ha." Pronunciation takes place deep at the back of your throat, and for correct pronunciation, one must constrict the back of the throat and exhale air while simultaneously saying "ha." In the program, this strong h ("ha") is emphasized whenever *ha, ah, hi, he,* or *hu* is encountered.

NOTE TO THE READER

The purpose of this book is merely to enable you to communicate in Omani Arabic. In the program itself (pages 17-38) you may notice that the composition of some of those sentences might sound rather clumsy. This is intentional. These sentences were formulated in a specific way to serve two purposes: to facilitate the easy memorization of the vocabulary and to teach you how to combine the words in order to form your own sentences for quick and easy communication, rather than making complete literal sense in the English language. So keep in mind that this is not a phrase book!

As the title suggests, the sole purpose of this program is for conversational use only. It is based on the mirror translation technique. These sentences, as well as the translations are not incorrect, just a little clumsy. Latin languages, Semitic languages, and Anglo-Germanic languages, as well as a few others, are compatible with the mirror translation technique.

Many users say that this method surpasses any other known language learning technique that is currently out there on the market. Just stick with the program and you will achieve wonders!

Note to the Reader

Again, I wish to stress this program is by no means, shape, or form a phrase book! The sole purpose of this book is to give you a fundamental platform to enable you to connect certain words to become conversational. Please also read the "Introduction" and the "About Me" section prior to commencing the program.

In order to succeed with my method, please start on the very first page of the program and fully master one page at a time prior to proceeding to the next. Otherwise, you will overwhelm yourself and fail. Please do not skip pages, nor start from the middle of the book.

It is a myth that certain people are born with the talent to learn a language, and this book disproves that myth. With this method, anyone can learn a foreign language as long as he or she follows these explicit directions:

* Memorize the vocabulary on each page

* Follow that memorization by using a notecard to cover the words you have just memorized and test yourself.

* Then read the sentences following that are created from the vocabulary bank that you just mastered.

* Once fully memorized, give yourself the green light to proceed to the next page.

Again, if you proceed to the following page without mastering the previous, you are guaranteed to gain nothing from this book. If you follow the prescribed steps, you will realize just how effective and simplistic this method is.

THE PROGRAM

Let's Begin! "Vocabulary" (Memorize the Vocabulary)

I | I am	Ana
With you	(Masculine) Ma'ak / (Fem) ma'ash
With him / with her	(m) ma'ah, (f) m'aha
With us	M'ana
For you	(Masc) halak intah /(Fem) halek inti
Without him / her	(m)bedono, (f)bedonha
Without them	Bedonhom
Always	Daiman
Was	Kan
This, this is, it's	Hatha
Today	El youm
Sometimes	Maraat
Maybe	Yemken
You, you are, are you?	(M) Intah (F) Intih
Better	Ahsan / BeKhir
You (plural)	(M) Ntouh / (F) intanh
He, he is	Howa
She, she is	Hiya
From	Min

Sentences from the vocabulary (now you can speak the sentences and connect the words)

This is for you
Hatha halak intah (m)
Hatha halak inti (f)
I am from Oman?
Ana min Oman
Are you from Muscat?
Intah(m)/Inti(f) min mascat?

I am with you
Ana m'aak
Sometimes you are with us at the market
Maraat inta M'ana fi as'souq
I am always with her
Ana daiman m'aha
Are you without them today?
Intah bedonhom el youm?

*In Omani Arabic, there are gender rules. Saying "for you" to a male is *halak inta*, but if you are talking to a female, it's *halak inti*. "This is for you" means it belongs to you and, hence, in this case we use *hatha halak*. However, if the sentence was "I did it for you" (i.e., I did this only because you are a special friend to me or because you mean a lot to me), here in this context we use *sawaytah halik* for the girl and *sawaytah halak* for the boy.

I was	Ana kent
To be	(M)Ashan Tkuun/(F)Ashan Tkuuni
The	El, ll, al
Same / like (*as in similar*)	Nafs / Methel
Good	Zain
Here	Hna
Very	Wagid
And	Wa / W
Between	Bayn
Now	Taw
Later / After / afterwards	Ba'den
If	Itha / La-w
Yes	Na'am / hiwa / heh
To	A'l / la / Ela
Tomorrow	Bukrah
Person	Shakhs / Flan
Also / too / as well	Ba'd

If it's between now and later
Itha kan bayn taw w ba'den
It's better tomorrow
Howa ahsan Bukrah
This is good as well
Hatha zain ba'd
To be the same person
Ashan Tkuun nafs elshakhes
Yes, you are very good
Hiwa, inta Wagid zain
I was here with them
Ana kent hna ma'hom
You and I
Inta w ana
The same day
Nafs el-yom

*In the Arabic language, adjectives usually proceed the noun. For example, "the same day" is *nafs el yom*, "small house" / *beit zagheer*, "tall person" / *shakhes taweel*, "short person" / *shakhes qa-seer*. There are exceptions, though. For example, when expressing admiration or something impressive, we can say, "How big is this house?" / *kam kuber hatha ll-beit?*

*In Omani Arabic there are two forms to signify "if" / *itha* and *la-w*. "If it's raining tomorrow, I am not going," for instance, in this case, we use "*itha.*" For "if I knew that this will happen, I wouldn't go to visit her," here the "if" is like "had I" and *la-w* will be used.

The Program

Me	Ni / li *(read footnote)*
Ok	Tamam/ ok
Even if	Hatta law
No	La'a
Worse	Akhas
Where	Wein
Everything	Killshi
Somewhere	Makan
What	Muh? / Aish?
Almost	Tq'riban
There	Henak
I go	Ana Arooh / Ana Aseer

Afterwards is worse
Ba'den Akhas
Even if I go now
Hatta law arooh taw
Where is everything?
Wein kilshi?
Maybe somewhere
Yimken fi makan
What? I am almost there
Muh? Ana Tq'riban Henak
Where are you?
(M) Inta wein? / (F) Inteh wein?

*In Arabic, the pronoun "me" has several definitions. In relation to verbs, it's *li* and it refers to any verb that relates to the action of doing something to someone, or for someone.
For example, "tell me," "tell (to) me" / *qool li*. *ni* just means "me": "love me" / *heb'ni* or "see me" / *shoof'ni* Other variations (eh): "on me" / *'ali*, "in me" / *fini*, **"mine"** / *mali*, "with me" / *ma'eh*, "in front of me" / *qeddameh*, "from me" / *minneh*.
*The same rule applies for "him" and "her"—both become suffixes: –h and –ha. Basically all verbs pertinent to males end with *h*, and all pertinent to female end with *ha*. For "them" put *hom*. For "us" put *na*. "love her" / *hebbha*, "love him" / *hebbh*, "love them" / *hebbhom*, "love us" / *hebbna*
Any verb that relates to doing something to someone, or for someone put *l*: "tell her" / *qoollha*, "tell him" / *qoollh*, "tell them" / *qoollhom*, "tell us" / *qoollna* Adding you as a suffix in Arabic is *ak* or *lak*, female *ik* or *lik*. "love you" / (M) *ahebbak*/ (F)*ahebbik*, "tell you" / (M) *aqoollak* / (F) *aqoollik*.

House	Beit
In, at, at the	Fi / fill
Car	Seyyara
Already	Aad
Good morning	Sabah el kheir
How are you?	(M) Keef halak? / (F) keef halik?
Where are you from?	(M) Inta min wein? / (F) inteh min wein?
Impossible	Mustaheel
Hello	Marhaba / hala
What is your name?	(M) muh ismak? / (F) muh ismik?
How old are you?	(M) kam omrak? / (F) kam omrik?
Son	'Eben
Daughter	Benet
To have	(M) 'Endoh / (F) 'Endha
Doesn't *or* **isn't**	Ma
Hard	Sa'ab
Still	Ba'ed
Then (or "so")	Ogub

She doesn't have a car, so maybe she is still at the house?
Heya ma 'endha seyyara, ogub yemkin heyeh ba'da fill beit?
I am in the car already with your son and daughter
Ana fill seyyara Aad ma'ah 'ebnak wa bentak
Good morning, how are you today?
Sabah el kheir, kef halak elyom?
Hello, what is your name?
Marhaba, muh ismak?
How old are you?
kam omrak?
This is very hard, but it's not impossible
Hatha wagid sa'ab, laken ma mustaheel
Then where are you from?
Eghab Inta min wein?

*In Arabic, possessive pronouns become suffixes to the noun. For example, in the translation for "your," *ak* is the masculine form, and *ik* is the feminine form.
  - "your book" / *ketabak* (m.), *ketabik* (f.)
  - "your house" / *beitak* (m.), *beitik* (f.)
*In the Arabic language, as well as in other Semitic languages, the article "a" doesn't exist. She doesn't have a car, *heya ma 'indha seyyara.*

Thank you	Shukran
For	La, ala
Anything	Ay-shi
That, That is	(M) Hatha / (F) Hathi
Time	Waq'et
But	Bas / Lakin
No/ Not	Ma, La'
I am not	Ana ma
Away	B'eed
Late	Mta'kher
Similar, like	(M) Nafsah / (F) nafs'ha
Another/ Other	Gheir/ thani
Side	Janeb/soub
Until	Hata
Yesterday	Ams
Without us	Min doun'na
Since	Min
Day	Yom
Before	Qabel

Thanks for everything
Shukran ala killshi
It's almost time
Huwa el waq'et Tq'riban
I am not here, I am away
Ana ma hina, ana b'eed
That is a similar house
Hatha beit nafsah
I am from the other side
Ana min el soub thani
But I was here until late yesterday
Laken ana kent hna elein Ams M'takhar
I am not at the other house
Ana ma fill beit ith-thani

*In Arabic there are 3 definitions for time:

-Time, *waqt* refers to; era, moment period, duration of time.
-Time(s), *marra(t)* refers to; occasion or frequency.
-Time, *sei'ah* in reference to; hour, what time is it.

*In Omani Arabic, there are two separate cases used to signify "side": *janeb* and *soub*. For "I am from the other side" *soub*, but for "I stand by your side" here "your side" is *janbak*.

*As regards to negotiations, in Omani Arabic either *la* or *ma* is used.
"No" / La
"I am saying no" / *Ana aqool la*.
Ma is used to represent "not," "don't," "doesn't," "isn't."
"I am not here" / *Ana ma hina*.

I say / I am saying	Ana aqool
What time is it?	Kam el waq'et?
I want	Ana areed / Ana baghee
Without you	(M) Min donok /(F) min donik
Everywhere /wherever	Kel makan / Ay makan
I am going	Ana Arooh /Ana Aseer
With	Ma'
My	y (read footnote)
Cousin	(S)(M) ben 'ammeh, (F)benet 'ammteh/(P) awlad 'ammeh, banat 'ammteh
I need	Ana Areed
Right now	Taw
Night	Leil
To see	Shoof
Light	Lait / daw
Outside	Barra
Without	Min don
Happy	Farhan
I see / I am seeing	Ana ashoof

I am saying no / I say no
Ana aqool la / Ana aqool la
I want to see this today
Ana Areed ashoof hatha il yom
I am with you everywhere
Ana ma'ak kel makan
I am happy without my cousins here
Ana Farhan min doon awlad 'ammeh hna
I need to be there at night
Ana Areed akoon hnak fill-leil
I see light outside
Ana Ashoof daw barra
What time is it right now?
Kam el seh'aa Taw?

*"Mine" / *mali* is also a possessive pronoun. *Mali* means "my" but also becomes a suffix to a noun. Nouns ending in a vowel end with *–y*. Nouns ending with a consonant end with *–y*. For example: "cousin" / *iben 'amm*, "my cousin" / *iben 'ammy*, "cup" / *koob*, "my cup" / *kooby*

*For second and third person masculine noun, *ibin* ("son"), male (S) *ak*, (P) *kom*, and female (S) *ik*, (P) *ken*. "His" – *h* / "hers" – *ha*, noun endings will be ah(for male) and ha (for female)."your son" / *ibnak* (m.), *ibnik* (f.), "your (plural) son" / *ibinkom* (m.), *bintkam* (f.), "his son" / *ibnah*, "her son" / *ibnha*, "our son" / *ibinn'a*, "their son" / *ibnohom*(m.), *ibnohen* (f.).

*For second and third person feminine noun: "car" / *seyyara*.
"your car" / *seyyartak*, "your (plural) car" / *seyyaretkom*, "his car" / *seyyartah*, "her car" / *seyyaretha*, "our car" / *seyyaretna*, "their car" / *seyyarethom* (m.), *seyyarethen* (f.).

* In the Omani dialect, *areed* is used to signify both the verbs "I want" and "I need."
*This *isn't* a phrase book! The purpose of this book is solely to provide you with the tools to create *your own* sentences!

The Program

Place	Makan
Easy	Ba-seet / khafeef / sahill
To find	L-qah
To look for/to search	Dor
Near / Close	Qareeb
To wait	Nte-der
To sell	Baya'a
To use	Sta'amill
To know	'Ariff
To decide	Qarir
Between	Bein
Next to	Ganeeb
To	La-ela *(place)*/ashan *(reason)*

This place it's easy to find
Hatha el makan sahilll telqah
I want to look for this next to the car
Ana areed A dor 'ala hatha ganeeb seyyara
I am saying to wait until tomorrow
Ana aqool nante-der ela bukra
This table is easy to sell
Hathi tawleh sahill baya'a
I want to use this
Ana areed ista'amill hatha
I need to know where is the house
Ana areed a'ariff wein el-beit
I want to decide between both places
Areed Aqarir bein el makanien

* For pronouns that are followed by a present tense verb, in the Omani dialect, some letters are added to the beginning of the verb or at the end. For example:
"To say" / *qool*
"I say" / *Aqool* - add *A*
"He says" / *Yqool* - add *Y*
"She says" / *Tqool* - add *T*
"You say" / *Tqool* (M) – *Tqooly* (F) - add *T* at the front for both and add *Y* at the end for female
"We say" / *Nqool* - add *N*
"They say" / *Yqoolo* - add *Y* at the front and *O* at the end
*When a pronoun is followed by a verb in series, we add the relevant letter to all of the verbs. For example,
"I want to go to school" / *Ana areed arooh el madrasah.*
"He wants to go and see a movie" / *Howa yreed yrooh yshoof falam.*
"They want to go and see a movie" / *Humah yreedo yrooho wa yshoofo falam.*
*Please pay close attention to the conjugation of verbs, whether they are in first person, second, or third. Unlike Anglo-Germanic languages, Latin languages, or even Classical Arabic, in which the first verb is conjugated and the following is always infinitive, in colloquial Arabic, it is quite different. The first verb is conjugated and the following one is conjugated as well. Keep in mind: The Omani dialect of the Arabic language is considered a colloquial, rather than an official language.

Because	La'annah
To buy	Shtreh
Life	'Omr, hayaht
Them, they, their	Hum'a
Bottle	Gharsha
Book	Ketab
Mine	Mali
To understand	Fham
Problem / Problems	(S) Mushkelah / (P) Mashakill
I do / I am doing	As'awi
Of	Min
To look	Shoof
Myself	Nafsi
Enough	Bas'h / khafi
Food / water	Akill / ma-yy
Each/ every/ entire/ all	Kill / killah
Hotel	Funduq

I like this hotel because I want to look at the beach
Ana aheb hatha fundoq la'annah Areed ashoof el-baharr
I want to buy a bottle of water
Ana areed ashtreh gharsha ma-yy
I do this every day
Ana as'awi hatha kill yom
Both of them have enough food
Al-ethnain end-hom akill kafi
That is the book, and that book is mine
Hatha huwweh l-kteib, w thak l-kteib mali
I need to understand the problem
Ana areed afham almushkilah
I see the view of the city from the hotel
Ana ashoof mandhar el madinah min el fundoq
I do my homework today
Ana as'awi el wageeb elyom
My entire life (all my life)
Kill 'omrih / kill hayahtih

*"Both of them" is *al-ethnain*.
*There are two ways of saying "life" in Arabic: *'omr* and *hayaht*.

I like	Ana ahebb
There is / There are	Henaak
Family / Parents	Ahley
Why	Laish
To say	Qool
Something	Shai
To go	Rooh
Ready	Gah-his
Soon	Qareeban
To work	Yshtighil
Who	Men
Busy	Mashghool
That (conjunction)	Annah
I Must	Lazim
Important	Mu-him

I like to be at my house with my parents
Ana ahebb akoon fill beyteh ma' ahley
I want to know why I need to say something important
Ana areed a'aref laish ana baghee aqool shai mu-him
I am there with him
Ana henak ma'ah
I am busy, but I need to be ready soon
Ana mashghool, bass ana baghee akoon jeh-his areeban
I like to go to work
Ana ahebb arooh ishte-ghill
'Who is there?
Men henaak?
I want to know if they are here, because I want to go outside
Ana areed a'aref itha huma hna, le annah ana areed arooh barra
There are seven dolls
Henaak saba' lu'baat
I need to know that it is a good idea
Ana areed a'aref annah hatha fekra zienah

*In the last sentence, we use "that" as a conjunction (*annah*) and a demonstrative pronoun (M) *hatha* / (F) *hatheh*.

How much /How many	Kam?
To bring	Jeeb
With me	Ma'eh
Instead	Badal
Only	Bas
When	Lamma / mata
I can / Can I?	Ana aroom (or) aq'der
Or	Aw
Were	Kanoo
Without me	Min douni
Fast	Bser'aa
Slow	Showayah
Cold	Bared
Inside	Dakhil
To eat	A'akhol
Hot	Sakhen
To Drive	Asooq'

How much money do I need to bring with me?
Kam feloos ana ajeeb ma'eh?
Instead of this cake, I want that cake
Badal hathi caikah, areed hathik el-caikah
Only when you can
Bas lamma taq'dar
They were without me yesterday
Kanoo min douni ams
Do I need to drive the car fast or slow?
Asooq el seyyara bser'aa aw showayah?
It is cold inside the library
Hwa bared dakhil el-maktabeh
Yes, I like to eat this hot for my lunch
Aywa, ana ahebb akhol hatha sakhen fill ghada
I can work today
Ana aqdar ashte-ghill elyom

*"Were" is *kano*, "we were" is *kenna*.
*"I can" and "can I?" could either be *ana aqder* or *ana aroom*. "You can" is teqder and "can you?" is also *teqder?*

The Program

To answer	Jahwibb
To fly	Teer
Time / Times	Marrah / Marrat
To travel	Safer
To learn	T'allam
How	Keef
To swim	Sbah
To practice	Timr'an
To play	L'aab
To leave (something)	Khaleh *(please read the footnote below)*
Many /much /a lot	Ktheer (or) wajeed
I go to	Ana arooh ela
First	Awwal
To leave (a place)	Khrig *(please read the footnote below)*
Around	Qareeb

I want to answer many questions
Ana areed ajahwibb ala as'ilah ktheerah
I must fly to Dubai today
Ana lazhim ateer ela Dubai elyom
I need to learn how to swim at the pool
Ana areed at'allam keef asbah fill houdh
I want to learn to play better tennis
Ana baghee at'allam al'aab tennis ahsan
I want to leave this here for you when I go to travel the world
Ana baghee akhalleh hatha hna lak lamma arooh asafer ela 'aalamm
Since the first time
Min awwal marrah
The children are yours
Hathola awladak

*In Omani Arabic; to leave (something) is *khali*. To leave (a place) is *khrig*.
*In Arabic there are 3 definitions for time:
-Time, *waqi't* refers to; era, moment period, duration of time.
-Time(s), *marra(t)* refers to; occasion or frequency.
-Time, *sa'a* in reference to; hour, what time is it.
*With the knowledge you've gained so far, now try to create *your own* sentences!

Nobody / Anyone	Ma-had / ay-had
Against	Dedd
Us	Nahhno
To visit	Zoor
Mom / Mother	Imm
To give	A'ateh
Which	Ayy
To meet	Telaqhi
Someone	Had
Just	Bas
To walk	Imshi
Week	Esboo'
Towards	Soub
Than	Min
Nothing	Ma-shi

Something is better than nothing
Shai ahsan min ma-shi
I am against him
Ana dedd-ah
Is there anyone here?
Ay-had hna?
We go to visit my family each week
Nehhna nrooh nzoor el ayleh kill esboo'
I need to give you something
Ana areed a'teek shi
Do you want to go meet someone?
Enta treed trooh Telaqhi had?
I was here on Wednesdays as well
Ana kent hna el arbe'aa ba'ad
Do you do this everyday?
Enta ta'mel hatha kill yom?
You need to walk around, but not towards the house
Enta a'laik timshi qareeb, bas ma soub el-beit

*In Arabic, when using the pronoun "you" as a direct and indirect object pronoun (the person who is actually affected by the action that is being carried out) in relation to a verb, the pronoun "you" becomes a suffix to that verb. That suffix becomes *ak* (masc.) *ik* (fem.). For example: "to give" / *a'teh*: "to give you" / *ta a'teek*, "to tell" / *qool*: "to tell you" / *qoolak* (m.), *qoolik* (f.), "to see" / *shoof*, "see you" / *shoofak*: "to see you" (plural) / *shoofkom* (m.), *shoofkan* (f.)
For third person male, add *ah* and *hom* for plural, for female add *ha* and *hen* for plural. For example: "tell him" / *qoolah*, "tell her" / *qoolha*, "see them" / *shoofhom* (m.), *shoofhen* (f.), "see us" / *shoofna*.

The Program

I have	'Endhi
Don't	Ma / La
Friend	Saheb, sadeeq
To borrow	Astaqreed
To look like / resemble	Ishbah
Grandfather	Gadd
To want	Treed
To stay	Ibqa
To continue	Kam'mill
Like (preposition)	Methel
Way	Tareeq
I don't	Ana la/ma
To show	Tshoof
To prepare	Tgahaz
I am not going	Ana ma arooh

Do you want to look like Salim?
Treed Tishbah Salim?
I want to borrow this book for my grandfather
Ana areed Astaqreed hatha el ketab la gaddy
I want to drive and to continue on this way to my house
Ana areed asooq wa akammill 'ala hatha tariq ela beity
I have a friend there, that's why I want to stay in Muscat
Endhi saheb henak, ashan ketha ana areed abqa fe mascat
I am not going to see anyone here
Ana ma rah ashoof ay-had hna
I need to show you how to prepare breakfast
Ana areed araweek keef Tgahaz reyouq
Why don't you have the book?
Laish ma 'indak el-ketab?
That is incorrect, I don't need the car today
Hatha ma saheeh, ana ma areed el seyyara elyom

*Ashan literally means "because" and "reason."

Conversational Arabic Quick and Easy

To remember	Tethakar
Your	Lak
Number	Raqum
Hour	Se'aa
Dark / darkness	Dalam
About / on the	Be / ala
Grandmother	Jaddah
Five	Khams
Minute / Minutes	Daqeqah / daqayeq
More	Akthar
To think	Fakker
To do	Sawy
To come	Ajy
To hear	Sma'
Last	Akhir
To talk / To Speak	Tekalam

You need to remember my number
Enta tehtag tit'hakar raqum-y
This is the last hour of darkness
hathy akher Se'aa min al dalam
I want to come and to hear my grandmother speak Arabic
Ana areed ajy w asma' jaddat-y tetkhlam 'arabi
I need to think more about this, and what to do
Ana areed afakker akthar fe hatha, w muh asawy
From here to there, it's only five minutes
Min hna ela henaak, hoa bas khams daqayeq
The school on the mountain
El madrasah ala ll jabal

*In Omani Arabic *fe* is used to signify "about." For example, "let's talk about this topic" / *ta'a netkalam fe ll moudou'* ... "On the mountain" is a place, so in this case, we will use *ala*.

*In Arabic with the question "is it?", the "it" can pertain to either a masculine or feminine noun. However, whenever pertaining to a masculine or feminine noun, it will become *howa* or *heyaa*. For example, when referring to a feminine noun such as sayaara ("the car"), "is it (the car in question) here?" / *heyaa hna?* When referring to a masculine noun such as kaleb ("a dog"), "is it (the dog in question) on the table?" *howa ala tawela?* For neuter, it's *hatha*. However, I yet again wish to stress that this isn't a grammar book!.

Early	Min waqet
To leave (to go)	Khrig/rooh
Again	marra thaniah
Arabic	Arabi
To take	A'khith
To try	Jarreb
To rent	Yista'jer
Without her	Min dounha
We are	Nahna
To turn off	Bannad
To ask	Tis'al / Titlib
To stop	Nwaqaf
Permission	Ethin
While	Lamma

He needs to leave and rent a house at the beach
Hoa yareed yarooh wa yista'jer biet ala shatti
I want to take the test without her
Ana areed a'khith el fahs min dounha
We are here a long time
Nahna hna min zaman
I need to turn off the lights early tonight
Ana areed abanad el laitat min waqet el leyleh
We want to stop here
Nahna nebgha Nwaqaf hna
We are from Oman
Nahna min Oman
The same building
Nafss el benayah
I want to ask permission to leave
Ana areed atlib ethin ashan arooh

*In Omani Arabic, "to stop" is *twaqaf*, but "to cease" is *khalas*. For example, if someone is bothering you, you tell them, "enough!" / *khalas*!

To open	Iftah
A bit, a little, a little bit	Shuwayyeh
To pay	Tidfa'
Once again	Marra thaniah
There isn't/ there aren't	Mashi
Sister	Okhte
To hope	Atmanna
To live (to exist)	A'Eesh
To live (in a place)	Saken
Nice to meet you	(M,F) Tsharrafna *(footnote)*
Name	Isem
Last name	Ism el qabylah
To return	Rrja'
America	Amrika
Door	Bab

I need to open the door for my sister
Ana areed aftah elbab hal okhte
I need to buy something
Ana areed ashtere shai
I want to meet your sisters
Ana areed aqaball okhtak
Nice to meet you, what is your name and your last name?
Tsharrafna, muh ismak wa isem qabyltak?
To hope for a little better
Atmanna enah Shuwayyeh ahsan
I want to return from the United States and to live in Oman without problems
Ana areed arja' min Amrika w a'esh fi Oman bla mashakill
Why are you sad right now?
(M)Laish inta hazeen taw? (F) Laish inti hazeenah taw?
There aren't any people here
Ma had hna
There isn't enough time to go to Salalah today
Ma shai waqet kafi ashan nroh ela Salala el yom

*In Omani Arabic, regarding the verb "to meet," there are two separate cases to define this verb: *tejtehme'* and *teqabil*, depending of the context. To meet for business is *tejtehme'*. To meet for getting acquainted is *teqabil*. In the sentence, "Do you want to go meet someone?" (the sister, getting acquainted with her), it's *teqabil*.
*In Omani Arabic, to indicate "nice to meet you" we use *tsharrafna*, however (M) *sharraftna* / (F) *sharraftina* can be used as well
*This *isn't* a phrase book! The purpose of this book is *solely* to provide you with the tools to create *your own* sentences!

To happen	Yestwi
To order	Tlob
To drink	Ishrab
Excuse me	Esmah li
Child	(M) Walad, (F) Bint
Woman	Hurma
To begin / To start	Bda
To finish	Khalas
To help	Sa'ed
To smoke	Dakhin
To love	Hebb
Afternoon	Assur

This must happen today
Hatha lazm yestwi el youm
Excuse me, my child is here as well
Esmah li, waldi hna ba'ad
I love you
Ana ahebbak
I see you
Ana ashofuk
I need you at my side
Ana areedak janbi
I need to begin soon to be able to finish at 3 o'clock in the afternoon
Ana areed abda qareeban ashan akhallas 'a sea'h thalathah el assur.
I need help
Ana areed musa'dah
I don't want to smoke once again
Ana ma areed adakhin marra thaniah
I want to learn how to speak Arabic
Ana areed at'allam keef atkalam 'arabi

*"To help" is *sa'ed*. However, "help!" is *musa'adeh*. "I need help" or "I need rescue" / *ana meh'taj musa'adeh*.
*"To be able to" is *ashan*.

To read	Qra
To write	Kteb
To teach	T'allem
To close	Sakkir
To choose	Khtar
To prefer	Faddill
To put	Hott
Less	Aqal
Sun	Shamess
Month	Shahar
I Talk	T'kalem
Exact	Zabt

I need this book to learn how to read and write in Arabic because I want to teach in the UAE
Ana areed hatha elketab ashan at'allam kif aqra w aktub bill-'arabieh la'ni areed 'allem fi Ll-Emarat

I want to close the door of the house
Ana areed asakkir bab el-beit

I prefer to put the gift here
Ana afaddill ahott el hadiyeh hna

I want to pay less than you for the dinner
Ana areed adfa' aqel minnak ala el 'asha

I speak with the boy and the girl in French
Ana At'kalem ma' el' walad wa ll bent bill fransi

There is sun outside today
Henak shamess barra elyom

Is it possible to know the exact date?
Mumkin a'rif etarikh be zabt?

Where is the airport?
Wein el matar?

I need to go to sleep now
Areed arouh anam taw

*"For the" is *el*
*"In" is *bill*
*With the knowledge you've gained so far, now try to create *your own* sentences!

The Program

To exchange (*money*)	Srof
To call	Tta-sill
Brother	Akho
Dad	Abo
To sit	Gles
Together	Ma' ba'dh
To change	Ghayyer
Of course	Akeed
Welcome	Ahlein
During	Waqet
Year/Years	(S)Sanah / (P)Seneen
Sky	Sama
Up	Foq
Down	Tahet
Sorry	A'ssif
To follow	Tba'a
To the	Ela
Big	Kbeer
New	Jedid
Never / ever	Abadan

I don't want to exchange this money at the bank
Ana ma areed asrof hatha el folous fill-bank
I want to call my brother and my dad today
Ana areed atta-sill be akhoy wa aboy el yom
Of course I can come to the theater, and I want to sit together with you and with your sister
Akeed ana aqdar ajy ela al massrah, wa areed agles Ma' ba'dh ma'ak w ma' okhtak
I need to go down to see your new house
Ana areed anzal ashan ashoof beytak el jdeed
I can see the sky from the window
Ana aqdar ashoof e'sama min el derishah
I am sorry, but he wants to follow her to the store
Ana a'seff, bass howa yereed yetb'ha ela ll mahal
I don't ever want to see you again
Ana ma areed abdan ashoofak marra thaniah

*In Omani dialect, brother is *akho*, and dad is *abo*. However, "my dad" is *aboy* and "my brother" is *akhoy*. "My sister" is *okhteh*, and "my mother" is *ommeh*.
*For the possessive pronouns, her (*ha*) and him (*ah*), both become suffixes to the verb or noun. Concerning nouns: her house / *beitha*, his house / *beitah*, concerning cases regarding verbs, please see footnotes on page 19.

To allow	Khallee
To believe	Saddeq
Morning	Sabah
Except	Ma-ada
To promise	Wa'd
Good night	Tisbah ala kheir
Each	Kill
People	Nas
To move (an object)	Nqol
To move (to a place)	Nqol
Far	Ba'eed
Different	Gheir
Man	Rejjal
To enter	Dkhol
To receive	Stelim
Quickly	Be'ser'a
Good evening	Masa al-kheir
Left / right	Yasar / yameen
Street	Shahri'

I need to allow him to go with us, he is a different man now
Ana areed asmah lah enah yrooh ma'na, howa rejjal gheir taw
I believe everything except this
Ana Asaddeq kill-shi ma'ada hathax
I promise to say good night to my parents each night
Ana Awa'dak ini aqool tisbah ala kheir le ahleh kill leyleh
The people from Jordan are very pleasant
El nas fill ordon waged taybeen
I need to find another hotel very quickly
Ana areed ahassal fundoq thani beser'a
They need to receive a book for work
Homa yereedo yistelmo ketab li esbou'
I see the sun in the morning
Ana ashoof eshamess fi sabah
The house is on the right side of the street
El beit ala yameen el shahri'

The Program

To wish	Tmanna
Bad	Ma-zien
To Get	Geeb
To forget	Nsa
Everybody / Everyone	Kill-had/ Kill-hom
Although	Hata-law
To feel	Hiss
Past	Madeiy
Next (following, after)	Gai
To like	Hebb
In front	Qiddam
Next (near, close)	Ganeb *(read the footnote)*
Behind	Wara
Well	Ahsan
Goodbye	Ma'-salamah
Restaurant	Mat'aam
Bathroom	Hammam

I don't want to wish you anything bad
Ana ma areed atmanna lak ayy-shi ma-zien
I must forget everybody from my past to feel well
Ana lazim insa kill-had min el madeiy hatta ahiss ahsan
I am next to the person behind you
Ana ganeb el shakhes elly warak
There is a great person in front of me
El shakhes elly qiddamy fannan
I say goodbye to my friends
Ana aqool ma'-salamah le as-haby
Where is the bathroom in the restaurant?
Wein el hammam fill mat'aam?
She has to get a car before the next year
Heya lazim tgeeb seyyara qabel el sanah el gaiah (f)
I like the house, but it is very small
Ana ahebb el beit, bass howa wageed zgheer

Ganeb literally means "side." In Arabic, it refers to "next." *ganeby* is "besides me" and *ganebak* is "besides you

To remove / to take out	Sheel
Please	Argok / law-samaht
Beautiful	(M)Heelo, (F)Heelwah
To lift	Sheel
Include / Including	Ma'
Belong	Makanah
To hold	Imsek
To check	T'akkad
Small	Zgheer
Real	Haqeeqy
Weather	Taqss
Size	Hagem
High	Irtifa'
Doesn't	Ma
So (as in then)	Eghab
So (as in very)	Wageed
Price	Qimah
Diamond	Mas

She wants to remove this door please
Heya treed tsheel hatha ll bab law-samaht
This doesn't belong here, I need to check again
Hatha ma makanah hna, ana areed at'akkad marra thaniah
This week the weather was very beautiful
Hatha Esbo'e el taqss kan wageed heelo
I need to know which is the real diamond
Areed a'raf ayy el almass haqeeqy
We need to check the size of the house
Nreed nit'akkad min hagem el beit
I want to lift this, so you need to hold it high
Ana areed asheel hatha, a'gab lazim Timsekah fooq
I can pay this even though that the price is expensive
Ana aqdar adfa' hatha hata-law innah el qimah ghaleh
Including everything is this price correct?
Ma' kill-shi hatha el qimah saheehah?

Countries of the Middle East
Bildan el-sharq el-awsatt

Lebanon	Lebnan
Syria	Suriya
Jordan	Ordon
Israel/Palestine/West Bank	Isra'eel/Felesteen/Deffah el-gharbeyyah
Iraq	Al-eraq
Saudi Arabia	So'odiyyah
Kuwait	Al-kuwait
Qatar	Qatar
Bahrain	Bahrein
United Arab Emirates	Al-Emarat
Oman	'Oman
Yemen	Yaman
Egypt	Massor
Libya	Leebya
Tunisia	Tunis
Algeria	Al-jaza'er
Morocco	Maghreb

Months

January	Yanayer
February	Febrayer
March	Mares
April	Ebril
May	Mayo
June	Yonio
July	Yolio
August	Aughustos
September	Septembar
October	Octobar
November	Novambar
December	Decambar

Days of the Week

Sunday	Ahad
Monday	Ethnein
Tuesday	Thulatha
Wednesday	Arbe'aa
Thursday	Khamees
Friday	Jom'aa
Saturday	Sabet

Seasons

Spring	Rabee'
Summer	Seif
Autumn	Khareef
Winter	Shehta'

Cardinal Directions

North	Shemal
South	Ganoob
East	Sharq'
West	Gharb

Colors

Black	(M)Aswad (F)Sawda
White	(M)Abyadd (F) Bayda
Gray	(M)Rmehdeh (F)Rmehdiyyah
Red	(M)Ahmar (F)Hamra
Blue	(M)Azraq (F)Zarqa
Yellow	(M)Asfar (F)Safra
Green	(M)Akhdar (F)Khadra
Orange	(M)Bertuqali (F)Bertuqaliah
Purple	(M)Banafsagy (F)Banafsagyah
Brown	(M)Bunneh (F)Bunniyyah

Numbers

One	Wahad
Two	Thnin
Three	Thalathah
Four	Arb'aah
Five	Khamsah
Six	Sittah
Seven	Sab'aah
Eight	Thamaniah
Nine	Tis'aah
Ten	'Ashrah

Twenty	'Eshreen
Thirty	Thalatheen
Forty	Arb'aa'een
Fifty	Khamseen
Sixty	Sitteen
Seventy	Saba'aeen
Eighty	Thamaneen
Ninety	Tisi'in
Hundred	Miyyah
Thousand	Alef
Million	Malyoon

CONCLUSION

Congratulations! You have completed all the tools needed to master the Saudi Gulf, Emirati, Qatari, Kuwaiti, Bahraini, and the Omani Arabic dialects, and I hope that this has been a valuable learning experience. Now you have sufficient communication skills to be confident enough to embark on a visit to the Gulf States impress your friends, and boost your resume so good luck.

This program is available in other languages as well, and it is my fervent hope that my language learning programs will be used for good, enabling people from all corners of the globe and from all cultures and religions to be able to communicate harmoniously. After memorizing the required three hundred and fifty words, please perform a daily five-minute exercise by creating sentences in your head using these words. This simple exercise will help you grasp conversational communications even more effectively. Also, once you memorize the vocabulary on each page, follow it by using a notecard to cover the words you have just memorized and test yourself and follow that by going back and using this same notecard technique on the pages you studied during the previous days. This repetition technique will assist you in mastering these words in order to provide you with the tools to create your own sentences.

Every day, use this notecard technique on the words that you have just studied.

Everything in life has a catch. The catch here is just consistency. If you just open the book, and after the first few pages of studying the program, you put it down, then you will not gain anything. However, if you consistently dedicate a half hour daily to studying, as well as reviewing what you have learned from previous days, then you will quickly realize why this method is the most effective technique ever created to become conversational in a foreign language. My technique works! For anyone who doubts this technique, all I can say is that it has worked for me and hundreds of others.

NOTE FROM THE AUTHOR

Thank you for your interest in my work. I encourage you to share your overall experience of this book by posting a review. Your review can make a difference! Please feel free to describe how you benefited from my method or provide creative feedback on how I can improve this program. I am constantly seeking ways to enhance the quality of this product, based on personal testimonials and suggestions from individuals like you.

Thanks and best of luck,

Yatir Nitzany

Made in United States
North Haven, CT
24 August 2024